4·90

Applied Linguistics and L...

GENERAL EDITOR: C. N. CANDLIN

WITHDRAWN

Applied Linguistics and Language Study

Advanced
Conversational English

DAVID CRYSTAL
DEREK DAVY

LONGMAN

LONGMAN GROUP LIMITED
Longman House
Burnt Mill, Harlow, Essex, UK

First published 1975
Fifth impression 1981

ISBN 0 582 55074 2

*We are grateful to the Firework Makers'
Guild for permission to reproduce the
drawing on page 27*

Printed in Hong Kong by
Wing King Tong Co Ltd

ISBN 0 582 56831 5 Tape (twin-track)

ISBN 0 582 79005 0 Cassette 1 × C90

Preface

This book represents a departure from the previous volumes in the *Applied Linguistics and Language Study Series*, in that the authors both characterize an applied linguistics problem and provide with their analysed data a set of practice materials which can be used by teachers and advanced learners, and which, importantly, can serve as models for further teacher-produced materials.

Recent concern with the nature of discourse has called further into question the oral dialogues of many ELT textbooks which, because of their sentence-structure illustrating task and a lack of ready-to-hand criteria for the treatment of actual speech, have borne little resemblance to the hesitations, false starts, speed and volume changing characteristics of everyday conversation. As a result, learners have been handicapped in their powers of interpretation of *real* spoken data, and have felt that their learning has not equipped them to seek the guidelines with which to steer a path through the oral jungle.

From this common experience, the authors set out to chart the nature of conversational speech, looking not only at the linguistic and phonetic markers to provide a clear classification, but also to indicate how these markers are typically employed sociolinguistically within the personal tactics of general conversational strategies. One can then discern from the wide variety of analysed and annotated extracts not only what typical intonations and conversational 'set phrases' actually occur, but what particular selections and co-selections can be made from the inventory for the particular ulterior conversational motives of the speaker.

The analysed and annotated extracts perform two important functions: firstly, they extend considerably our knowledge of the distinctive features of conversational English. It is no longer possible to relegate 'well . . .' to the category of a 'meaningless element', or simply to state that its frequent occurrence in speech is one way that speech is distinguished from writing. There are several 'well'-like items—'you know, I mean, sort of, kind of,' etc., and the authors suggest and exemplify what their meanings can be within discourse, and indicate, too, that we are only beginning to chart what turns out to be a highly complex area of English in use. Secondly, the example materials admirably serve the purpose of 'developing appropriate response behaviour in conversational interaction, for which the development of receptive, or interpretative abilities in language is the first essential stage'. Moreover, as the authors make clear in their final chapter, these analysed materials have a productive function in suggesting ways in which teachers may develop further exercises in the analysis of conversation for their own learners.

Above all, the book indicates in a clear analytical way what 'happens' in conversation as such, and it supports a growing concern that learning materials which have communication as their aim should themselves be based on accurately reported models with essential features distinctively highlighted.

Christopher N Candlin
General Editor
May 1975

Contents

Introduction

We first became aware of the need for information about informal conversational English as a result of our experiences on English language teaching courses and summer schools abroad. There we met many teachers and advanced students who had a good command of formal English, but who were aware that there existed a conversational dimension to the language that they had little experience of, and who expressed dissatisfaction with the kind of English they were regularly encountering in their coursework. Despite all the available materials, the request to 'say some real English into my tape-recorder' was disconcertingly persistent. It was more in evidence in those parts of the world which have little regular contact with English-speaking areas, such as South America, but we have come across a comparable demand in many parts of Europe too. In a way, the original motivation for this book was to present a compilation of material which would avoid the inconvenience and artificiality of the 'talk into the tape-recorder' exercise. It is more than this now, as we have included, in addition to the basic data, commentaries, analyses, general discussion, and suggestions for extension. But the basic aim is the same —to help students who feel they have a grasp of the structural patterns and usage of their regular coursework, and who want to develop their abilities in comprehension and fluency by using informal conversation as a model.

We began in early 1971. The delay has been largely due to the difficulty of obtaining natural conversational data in good recording conditions, dealing with ranges of subject-matter likely to be of interest to students of English. As one might expect, we had to record many hours of conversation before we could make a final selection which preserved this balance between spontaneity, recording quality, and interest. We attach particular importance to the naturalness of our data, which has not been edited in any way. We have not come across commercially available material that is so informal or realistic, and it is in this respect that we hope the main contribution of this book will lie. We see *Advanced Conversational English* as a source book of information about the standard educated colloquial language. It is not designed as a teaching handbook. For one thing, we are ourselves unclear as to how data of this kind can best be used in a teaching situation. We are aware that colloquiality sparks off attitudes about when, how, and how much it should be taught—or whether it can be formally taught at all. We have had relatively little experience of these matters; consequently we have restricted the teaching section of this book to some general remarks and suggestions about how the data might be approached. To develop real productive and receptive fluency in this area is a task yet to be thoroughly investigated by teachers and applied linguists. But we are clear about one thing: no progress will be made towards an improved ELT pedagogy without a clear understanding of the realities of English conversation. For too long, English language teachers have been operating with a stereotype of conversation: whether it proves best to stay working with this stereotype or not, it is time to develop a more accurate perspective about conversational structures and usage, within which such matters can be properly evaluated.

The collection of data of which our extracts form a part is now housed at University College London, in the files of the Survey of English Usage, which is financed by a grant from the Leverhulme Trust and the Calouste Gulbenkian Foundation.

Many people have helped us in the preparation of this book—not least our anonymous conversationalists, and the many teachers of English in this country and abroad on whom the extracts and the accompanying analyses were first tried out. We are grateful to all of them, and particularly to Brian Abbs, Christopher Candlin, Peter Clifford, and David Wilkins, for advice on specific pedagogical issues while the book was being written.

DC, DD
July 1974

1

Conversational English

The idea for this book arose out of an awareness that currently available English language teaching materials have not as yet bridged the gap between classroom English and English in use. It is clear that there are many excellent courses which help students to get through the introductory stages of learning the language; but there are few which have attempted to go beyond this point, and those which do so fall far short, in our opinion, of the goal of making students encounter and participate in the normal language of conversational English. The intermediate or advanced learner, typically, is aware that his English differs from the norms adopted by native speakers, but he finds little guidance as to how he can achieve a closer approximation to these norms. Often, indeed, he finds it extremely difficult to obtain any samples of conversational English at all to study, and even if he does, they will be unlikely to have accompanying analyses, commentary, or drills.

This state of affairs is not the learner's fault. The reasons for it are bound up with the stage which language-study has reached at the present time, and are part of a more general neglect of conversational norms in English language studies. There are, after all, two main difficulties over obtaining information about these norms. The first of these is that accumulating usable and reliable samples of natural, everyday, informal conversation is by no means easy. The problems embrace the technical (ensuring satisfactory recordings), the linguistic-psychological (for instance, ensuring that the speech is natural), and the legal (avoiding the many problems involved in publishing such material). Secondly, once one has accumulated such samples, there arise the difficulties of analysing them. The kind of English found in these samples is in many respects quite different from the kind confidently analysed in the standard textbooks and manuals (as we shall see); consequently, a great deal of analysis has to be carried out before pedagogically useful generalizations can be made. As a result, it takes many years of experience in collecting and analysing material of this kind before one can speak confidently about informal conversation; and it is for this reason that little has been done. In this book, we are relying very much on our experience of analysing English in connection with the Survey of English Usage at University College London, and related projects; and we hope that we have therefore been able to make some headway into these problems. But it is only a beginning.

There are a number of general comments which have to be made by way of introduction to the data and approach of this book. The main aim, as already suggested, is to provide samples and analyses of 'natural, everyday, informal conversation', and to make suggestions as to how this material might be pedagogically used. But what is meant by this label? We might simply have talked about 'conversation' throughout; but we feel that this term, on its own, is too vague and broad to be helpful. After all, it may be used to refer to almost any verbal interchange, from casual chat to formal discussion; hence we have used the term 'informal conversation', to emphasize which end of the conversational spectrum we are concerned with—conversation on informal occasions, between people who know each other, where there is no pressure from outside for them to be self-conscious about how they are speaking. What happens when people simply want to talk in a friendly relaxed way? The result is very different from what introductory textbooks about conversation usually lead one to expect, both in subject-matter and construction. And, for the foreign learner who finds himself a participant in such informal situations, there are immediately problems of comprehension and oral fluency.

Let us look in a little greater detail at the kinds of difference which distinguish what we see as the average textbook situation from what we find in our recorded conversations. We do not wish to be gratuitously critical of available teaching materials, from whose study we have profited a great deal. We simply wish to underline the important fact, often overlooked by students of English, that even the best materials we have seen are far away from that real, informal kind of English which is used very much more than any other during a normal speaking lifetime; and if one aim of the language-teaching exercise is to provide students with the linguistic expertise to be able to participate confidently and fluently in situations involving this kind of English, then it would generally be agreed that this aim is not being achieved at the present time. The extent of the difference may be informally appreciated by observing the reactions of many foreign students when they first step off the boat or plane in an English-speaking country, and find that acclimatization applies as much to language as to weather! It surprises many to realize that most people do not speak like their teacher, or their local British Council officers at cocktail-parties, and that there is far more variation in the standard forms of the language than their textbooks would lead them to expect.

If one thinks for a moment of the specimens of English which the learner is often presented with under the heading of 'conversation', it is difficult to avoid the conclusion that they are highly stylized— stiff imitations of the dynamic spontaneity of real life. With few exceptions, the language of tape-recorded dialogues is controlled, relatively formal, and articulated clearly by fluent professionals, either phoneticians or actors, reading from scripts. The characters which are developed in textbook families are nice, decent, and characterless; the situations in which they find themselves are generally unreal or dull. People in textbooks, it seems, are not allowed to tell long and unfunny jokes, to get irritable or to lose their temper, to gossip (especially about other people), to speak with their mouths full, to talk nonsense, or swear (even mildly). They do not get all mixed up while they are speaking, forget what they wanted to say, hesitate, make grammatical mistakes, argue erratically or illogically, use words vaguely, get interrupted, talk at the same time, switch speech styles, manipulate the rules of the language to suit themselves, or fail to understand. In a word, they are not *real*. Real people, as everybody knows, do all these things, and it is this which is part of the essence of informal conversation. The foreign learner will of course be quite conversant with these features from his native language already; it is part of our purpose to extend his feel for such matters in English.

Of course, it is not easy to make classroom dialogues real in the early years of learning a language. If you have learned but a few hundred words, and a small number of grammatical structures, then naturally dialogues are likely to be pale reflections of conversational reality—though even here something can be done to improve things, as we shall later suggest. This is not the range of language learning that we are primarily talking about. We are more concerned with those students who would have become advanced practitioners of English if they had had any advanced materials to assist them— students who have already completed the half-dozen books or so of a published course, and who may have passed a basic examination in English language use. These are students who want to bridge the gap between the relatively measured, synthetic utterances of the classroom and the spontaneous exchanges of everyday conversational life. Often, the learner is given the impression that all he has to do to achieve the goal of fluent connected speech is simply increase the quantity and speed of production of the structures already learned. But fluency here involves far more than merely stringing together the sentence-structures and patterns of pitch movement that have been picked up during the previous years of learning the language. A qualitative difference is involved, as we shall see. The point is one which many learners of English come to appreciate through bitter experience.

What we mean by qualitative differences can be illustrated very easily. The many kinds of linkage which sentences display—using pronouns, articles, adverbials, lexical repetitions, and so on—which are not relevant to the study of a sentence seen in isolation: this is one kind of structural modification which has to be considered. Another involves intonation. Having learned of the existence of six or so major types of tone-unit in English, the student must now learn that putting them together into acceptable sequences—to express parenthesis, or emphasis, for instance—involves his using a quite separate range of pronunciation features. A third example would be the need to develop the skill of knowing what to leave *out* of a sentence, or what can be taken for granted in a dialogue. To take a simple case, one should be aware that permissible answers to the question 'Where are you going tomorrow?' include the following: 'I'm going to the library', 'To the library', 'The library', and 'Library'. Sometimes it does not particularly matter which answer is chosen; but at other times a careless choice can produce an unintentional and embarrassing stylistic effect—as when the last of these is used with a clipped intonation pattern, giving an impression of impatience, and perhaps leading to the interpretation 'Mind your own business'. We do not wish to over-rate the nature of the problems involved in these examples of connected speech; but we do want to avoid the opposite impression, that there are no problems at all. As so often in language learning, recognizing the existence of a problem is the first step along the road to its solution.

There is another way in which we can draw attention to the gap that has to be bridged. We are of the opinion that introductory courses do not, on the whole, teach the student how to *participate* in a conversation. They do not attempt to increase his skills systematically in the whole range of behavioural cues which help effective social interaction, some of which are visual and tactile, as well as linguistic. For instance, it is uncommon to find any systematic attempt to introduce information about facial expressions and bodily gestures into a language-teaching course, even today, despite the fact that research in social psychology and elsewhere has shown very clearly that inter-cultural differences in such features are much greater than used to be supposed, and that the number of variables of this kind which can change the 'meaning' of a piece of social interaction within a single culture is considerable. Here are some typical linguistic issues involved in effective communication in dialogue, and which cause problems of the kind that we think an English course should attempt to answer. How do you hesitate in English? Are there different kinds of hesitation which have different meanings? Does facial expression affect the interpretation of intonation? (The answer is 'yes' to both of these questions.) How do you indicate that you would like to speak if someone else is already speaking? Or (more to the point) how do you do this politely? Here is an example in more detail. A foreigner may think that he can relax in a conversation while the English participant is talking—but nothing is further from the truth. On the contrary, full participation in a conversation requires continual alertness. Normal conventions require the person not doing the talking to nonetheless keep up a flow of brief vocalizations, such as 'm', 'mhm', and so on. If you do not use these responses, the person talking will begin to wonder whether you are still paying attention, or if you are being rude. If you use too many, the impression may be one of overbearing pugnacity or of embarrassing friendliness (depending on your facial expression). And if you put them in the wrong places, you may cause a breakdown in the intelligibility of the communication. For instance, if the speaker pauses after the definite article in the following sentence, as indicated by the dash, a 'm' inserted at this point is likely to sound quite inappropriate 'You see it's the—exercise that's the problem'. If you use a falling tone (especially the type which falls from high to mid in pitch, used to express non-committal sympathy), the speaker is likely to be puzzled, not having said anything to be sympathized with yet, and he may get the impression that you are so anxious to break in that you can't bear to wait for him to say it. And if you give an encouraging rising tone to the vocalization, you would sound like a television interviewer prompting him to speak—which he might not appreciate!

Now such information is really rather elementary—in the sense that it is so basic to the relative success or failure of conversational interaction that it could usefully be brought into any language-teaching course from the very beginning. If beginners were exposed more to real conversation, it might be argued, they would have less to 'un-learn' in later years. They might not understand the whole of every conversation with which they were presented, naturally; but they would at least begin the long process of developing their intuitions about rhythm, tone of voice, speed of speaking, gesture, and all the features of conversational strategy belonging to English, which, if left until much later, tend never to be acquired satisfactorily at all. There is some sense in the idea that one of the very first things to learn in a foreign language is how to hesitate in it —after all, when trying to remember a particular word or phrase, rather than display an embarrassed and sometimes misleading silence, an appropriate hesitant noise or phrase can be extremely effective in averting a total communicational breakdown. And we would also argue the need for early introduction of information about facial expressions, basic intonation tunes, response vocalizations, and so on, largely on the grounds that it will take longer to develop automatic reactions in these things than in the more familiar levels of linguistic structure. But whether elementary or not, the fact of the matter is that on the whole this kind of information is not brought into courses as they exist at present. The reason for this state of affairs has already been indicated: authors as well as students are aware of the problem, but until very recently, the basic research needed to isolate and define the range and complexity of these factors had simply not been done, and it always takes years for fundamental research to percolate into the classroom. Paradoxically, then, such 'elementary' information has to be permitted into our supposedly 'advanced' book.

We do not of course want to give the impression, in saying this, that the solutions to all the problems are known, or are easy. There are still many aspects of English intonation, for instance, about which very little is known. And while we are demanding that more attention be paid to the subject of real connected speech, and all that goes with it, in course-work, we are not yet in a position to outline the full list of rules which will permit the learner to construct all types of connected discourse from a knowledge of the structures of individual sentences. Research into the matter is going on in many centres now. But enough precise information has already been gathered together to enable a start to be made, and it is this which we are attempting to do here. In this book, we shall restrict ourselves to issues where there is fairly wide agreement about the facts, concentrating in particular on the more central areas of conversational syntax, vocabulary and phonology. We shall occasionally introduce the tentative results of recent research, but whenever we are not sure of the general applicability of some work, we shall say so.

Another impression which we do not want to give is that failure to know and use features of conversational interaction and connected speech such as we illustrate in this book will inevitably result in the foreign learner being unintelligible to or criticized by native speakers. We are *not* suggesting that unless the student can hesitate properly in English, he might as well give up in the expectation that a terrible fate will befall him when he steps off the boat! The features taught in this book, once mastered, will produce more successful and fluent conversation, we claim, but not all of them are absolutely essential to comprehension and intelligibility (those which *are* particularly important we shall discuss at length). Moreover, some of the features we shall talk about many foreigners will know already, as there may be little difference in their use in the foreign language. This will be particularly so for students who speak languages closely related to English, or where there has been a high level of cultural contact. There are *relatively* few intonational differences between Spanish and English, for instance, that cause serious problems of intelligibility— and before the Spanish reader reaches for his pen in protest, let him think for a moment of the vast intonational differences that separate English from Japanese, which make the Spanish/English contrasts seem small by comparison. Similarly, it is not going to be a disaster if a French or German student inserts his own language's agreement noises into a conversation in English—after all, generations of students have been doing just this with apparent success.

But for those students who want more than simply to 'get by', who want to develop a confident command of the language they use, who want to know precisely what they are doing in a conversation and what effect it is likely to have—for these students, a great deal more than intuition is required. For them, lack of any basic training in what we might call 'English sociolinguistic technique' is one of the biggest stumbling blocks of all in developing a satisfactory conversational manner. Regardless of the closeness or otherwise of the foreigner's culture to English, there exist many problems, of different orders of difficulty, which have to be mastered if the goals of confident and effective communication are to be reached. A fairly well-known example is the means used in order to get a conversation started at all in English. 'Talking about the weather' is not as widespread as is sometimes believed. What ranges of subject-matter *may* be used, then, if you want to start a conversation with a stranger? In some cultures, the permissible 'opening gambit' is very different from the type available in English. In at least one culture, for instance (which we shall keep nameless), we are told that it is the expected thing, upon entering a house, to enquire about the cost of the soft furnishings—hardly an appropriate topic for England! In a similar way, commenting on the excellence of the food is an *expected* response when invited home for a meal with an English family: it would be inappropriate, to say the least, to sit through the whole of a meal preserving a stony silence about its quality—but to comment about the food being eaten seems positively rude to many foreigners, who would never do such a thing in their own culture. Transferring one's own cultural sociolinguistic habits to English is the easiest thing in the world to do without realizing that anything is wrong, because the responses are so automatic and apparently unstructured. And as this kind of error has nothing obviously to do with interference problems of grammar, vocabulary, or pronunciation, the danger is that the native speaker's reaction to a blunder here will be to assume that it is the foreigner himself who is *deliberately* being rude, or provocative. This difficulty has long been recognized in intonation studies: unlike grammar, vocabulary, and segmental pronunciation, mistakes in intonation are not usually noticed and allowed for by native speakers, who assume that in this respect a person sounds as he means to sound. 'That chap has some interesting things to say, but he's so arrogant about it all' may be a reaction to a foreigner who has little control over his low rising tones, for instance. This kind of unconscious brick-dropping is, we know, extremely common; and its eradication should be a main aim of any approach to the teaching of conversation.

It seems to us that in order to participate effectively in a conversation in English, the foreigner needs to be fully aware of the implications of two quite distinct issues. First, he needs to be totally 'in tune' with the behaviour, language patterns and presuppositions of whoever he is talking to and with the social situation in which the conversation is taking place. And secondly, he needs to be able to respond to all of this in the appropriate way, using language along with other forms of behaviour. Both these issues are complex, and in this book we shall concentrate largely on the problem of 'getting into tune'. Here there is clearly an overlap with the traditional notion of 'comprehension', but 'being in tune' involves far more than understanding the logical and grammatical structure of a conversation and the vocabulary contained therein. It means, for instance, being able to identify any linguistic or social distinctiveness in the other participant's speech or general behaviour. It means being able to recognize from someone's accent that he is (say) from America—if only to avoid unintentionally making rude remarks about Americans in the course of the conversation! It means recognizing when you have offended someone, by noting the change in the 'tone' of the conversation. It means recognizing when people are being natural, or formal; knowing when to laugh and when not to laugh; and so on. It also means being able to continue with the kind of difficult conversation in which background noise interferes—as at a railway station, or when listening to someone with a cold. These are all part of 'being in tune'. They amount to what we would call a 'receptive fluency' or 'command' of English. Ideally, the competent foreigner should be able to deal with the same range of linguistic variation as the native speaker. Approximations to this ideal will of course depend on a variety of factors, of which motivation is perhaps the most important; but there is little point, it seems to us, to set our language learning sights any lower than equivalence with the native speaker, and it is his familiarity with a range of linguistic distinctiveness which we are trying to capture in this book.

We know that the foreign learner is never presented with this whole range of usage, and he is certainly never guided through it. We can look at it as an aspect of the unpredictability which any communication situation presents, and which any foreigner, as soon as he steps off the boat or plane, may expect to encounter. Speaking to a porter on a railway station, all foreign learners find, is a far cry from the calm atmosphere of the classroom, and the familiar accents of one's teacher and classmates. Nor is it solely a question of accent. It is a fundamental change from a pedagogically orientated world, in which people make allowances for mistakes and incomprehension, to a world of a quite different character. In class, if a point is not understood, the teacher will almost certainly carry out some recapitulation. In real life, this sometimes happens, but usually people are in too much of a hurry to make allowances or recapitulate, and they rarely attempt to be fully explicit. In giving street directions to an enquirer for instance, the speed of speech is far greater than that normally used in classroom work, and any requests for a reduction in speed are often thought to come from a lack of intelligence rather than a lack of linguistic practice. (A similar state of affairs is discovered by many English school leavers in the process of moving from school to job; this is not solely a foreigner's problem.) Or again, a speaker's presuppositions may make his responses largely unintelligible, as in: 'You don't want to turn left at the end of that street, 'cos of the cricket'. Here the intermediate stages in the argument are passed over in silence, namely, that this is the time that the crowds watching the cricket match will be leaving the ground and thus causing congestion, which the enquirer ought to avoid. There are many problems of this kind, as we shall see. Moreover, this is a peculiarly advanced difficulty. As your ability in a foreign language improves, there seems to come a stage when the better you are, the worse the problems become! The reason is simple. If your English is awful, then it's obvious; and if you can find a nice enough person to talk to, a pleasant enough (albeit chaotic) dialogue will ensue. But if your English is quite good, and especially if you don't look particularly foreign, the native speaker will assume you are like he is, and will talk accordingly. This is the problem period, when production ability is a false guide to overall comprehension, and it is a stage at which a great deal of practice is needed. It is unfortunately a stage which seems to be given little attention in the language-teaching literature.

As a last example of the kind of bridging of gaps which must be done in developing receptive fluency, we would point to the need to recognize deviations from linguistic norms as well as the norms themselves. One assumption we work on here, of course, is that on the whole people want to be friendly; they want to get on well with others, which involves telling jokes, making pleasantries, and the like. And the point is that a good deal of everyday humour, as well as much of the informality of domestic conversation, relies on deviance from accepted norms of one kind or another. Person A may adopt a 'posh' tone of voice in making a point to B; he may deliberately speak in an archaic, or religious, or journalistic way to get a particular effect; or he may extend a structural pattern in the language further than it is normally permitted to go—as when, on analogy with 'three hours ago' one might say 'I said that to you three buses ago'. All this might be referred to as 'stylistic' variation (using a rather restricted sense of 'stylistic' here), and in a way parts of our book might be considered as an extended exercise in applied stylistics. The aim, however, is more precisely stated by saying that the intention of the book as a whole is to develop appropriate response behaviour in conversational interaction, for which the development of receptive, or interpretative abilities in language use is the first, essential stage. In the present case, we are of the opinion that information about types of deviance is particularly crucial in foreign language teaching. It is always especially embarrassing when a foreigner fails to see the point of a simple joke, does not join in the smiles of a group because his comprehension is lagging behind, or unintentionally makes a joke himself (being unaware of a pun, for instance)— and in all this a keen awareness of the native's deviant usage is very often what is lacking.

2

The Conversational Extracts

Thus far we have been talking very generally about the extent to which language-teaching pays insufficient attention to norms of informal conversational English. We have suggested that the main reason for difficulty is the unavailability of teaching material based on data that accurately reflect these norms. Consequently our aim now is to present a range of extracts from which it will be possible to illustrate in detail the features of conversation that we consider to be important. These extracts are taken from a series of conversations on a variety of occasions and topics, using many different speakers from varied backgrounds. The salient points about this material which differentiate it from most of the recorded conversations that are commercially available are twofold: (a) it is spontaneously produced utterance, no scripts or other written cues being involved in its production; (b) it is representative of a range of colloquial usage which avoids the formal levels of discussion or debate, concentrating instead on the kind of language that is naturally used between people of similar social standing when talking about topics of common interest on informal, friendly occasions.

In order to obtain material which is as natural as possible, we have recorded the conversations in a normal domestic environment, not in a studio. We hope we have achieved a good recording quality while retaining those incidental noises without which any conversational interaction would begin to sound somewhat unnatural. In over half of the conversations the speakers were not aware that they had been recorded, permission to use the material being obtained from them afterwards. For the remainder of the material the speakers were aware of the presence of the microphone, but in every case the recording was made some time after the start of the conversation when behaviour had become thoroughly relaxed. On the basis of the analyses that we have done (see Chapter 3), we have been unable to find any marked difference between the language of the two types of extract, and have accordingly treated them as homogeneous.[1]

The tape accompanying this book contains fifteen extracts totalling some 40 minutes. In our discussion, we shall sometimes go beyond this basic data, and bring in examples of usage from elsewhere; but most of our attention will centre on the language these samples contain. It is therefore important to listen to these samples, more than once if necessary, while working through the analytical section of the book in Chapter 3. The details of the background to each extract are given before the transcription in the following pages. We have selected extracts which contain subject-matter likely to be of general interest to the foreign learner while at the same time being directly concerned with matters arising out of English culture and everyday life in Britain. We have also concentrated on the kind of British English likely to be familiar to most learners, and most of the participants use one of that range of accents, generally referred to under the heading of 'received pronunciation', which is the most widely known and used in parts of the world where language-teaching influence has been predominantly British.

Each extract is accompanied by a commentary, which deals with points of pronunciation, syntax, lexis and usage which might cause temporary difficulties of interpretation as one listens to the conversation. The commentary should be read in relation to the transcribed text before moving on to the analysis section of the book. But it is beneficial, we feel, to listen to the tape-recordings *before* making any detailed study of the transcription and the commentary—or even seeing the transcription at all—as it is only in this way one can arrive at an accurate impression of listening comprehension ability when put into contact with material of this kind. The procedure we expect to be most widely useful in the study of each extract is as follows:

Stage One: Read the introduction to an extract.

Stage Two: Listen to the corresponding taped extract, without looking at the printed text.

Stage Three: Listen to the tape again, simultaneously following the printed text.

Stage Four: Read through the text, along with the commentary.

Stage Five: Listen to the tape once more, again without looking at the text.

1. For readers who may be interested in comparing the two types from other points of view, it may be worth noting that Extracts 1, 4, 7, 8, 9, 11, 12, 13 and 15 involve speakers who were unaware of being recorded.

Different teaching-situations will of course invite alternative procedures.

Each extract is printed with a transcription which indicates the main prosodic features used by the speakers. We are using 'prosodic features' here in a general sense to include all vocal effects due to variations in pitch ('intonation'), loudness ('stress'), speed, rhythm and quality of speaking—this latter label subsuming all that is usually loosely gathered under the heading of 'tone of voice'. All the main variations of these kinds which correlate with contrasts in the meaning of a sentence (e.g. its attitudinal force, its stylistic effect, its grammatical analysis) are indicated in the transcription.

It is not necessary to learn the whole of the transcription system in advance of studying the texts. Increased auditory familiarity with the tape-recordings, along with simultaneous reading, will produce an ability to interpret the main features of the transcription in due course. And whenever it is important to focus on a prosodic effect in the section below, we shall be providing a general description of the effect in the commentary, by way of clarification. However, to learn to use a prosodic transcription can be very helpful, in that it can help to identify specific contrasts which may be causing difficulties of interpretation, and also be a way in which awareness of the patterns present in these texts may be more readily extended to the analysis of English usage in general. The transcription, and the terminology which accompanies it, is simply a way of talking about an unfamiliar but fundamental area of English usage. How complex it seems to you will depend on how much previous experience you have had in reading and using phonetic transcriptions, or linguistic symbolism of any kind.

We have tried to minimize difficulty in this matter by printing the extracts in ordinary spelling and not in phonetic or phonemic transcription in order to make them more immediately easy to read for the many advanced students who have not been trained to use a full transcriptional system, but who at the same time are able to read normal English orthography fluently. In effect, we are assuming that students at this level will in any case know how to pronounce the words contained in the extracts, and that there is nothing to be gained by printing these in phonemic script. This of course means that we can no longer make explicit the whole range of assimilations and elisions which characterize so much of connected speech; but wherever particularly interesting problems arise, the student will find that these are given adequate attention in the commentaries. We also devote the pronunciation section of the analytic discussion in Chapter 3 to this point. The only times we actually use a phonemic transcription in the texts is to indicate misarticulated or unidentifiable lexical items.[1]

Our principle, then, is to make use of ordinary orthography as far as possible. However, this principle cannot extend to the use of normal punctuation, as this is an extremely poor reflection of the prosodic features of speech, which are so essential for satisfactory comprehension. We have therefore developed a system of notation which enables us to mark in each prosodic feature as it occurs, and this is what accounts for any unfamiliarity in the appearance of the extracts below. It will be found, however, that it is perfectly possible to read through the extracts with ease, if certain points are borne in mind. The main thing to be aware of is that the prosodic transcription does not have to be assimilated all at once. All prosodic features are important, since they can all alter the meaning of a sentence; but some features are much more important than others. Altering one prosodic effect to another may at times produce a startling change of meaning; but at other times the effect may be so subtle that the listener hardly notices, except perhaps to have an uncomfortable feeling that something different has happened. The prosodic effect which underlies the vivid description 'An ironic note crept into his voice' is extremely subtle, compared with that which underlies such attitudes as anger or puzzlement, for example. In our transcription, we have tried to 'grade' the importance of the prosodic effects by using the range of typographic devices we had at our disposal. To get the 'basic' meaning of the transcribed sentences, then, it is not essential for the student to laboriously work through the entire transcription; all he need do is be clear about the basic conventions of *layout*, *pause marking*, *intonational organization*, and *general direction of pitch movement*. If a prosodic effect not falling under these headings turns out to be of crucial importance for the basic interpretation of the utterance, then, of course, we shall say so.

Layout

The speakers are named in order of speaking, A, B, C, etc., and at a change of speaker the transcription commences a new line. Whenever one speaker begins to speak while the other is already speaking, the

1. Here, as elsewhere in this book, the phonemic symbols we use correspond with those given by Gimson (1970).

overlapping utterances are printed one beneath the other. For example, in the following, speaker A says 'wasn't it' at the same time as speaker B says 'all the':

A   that was a bit early wasn't it

               all the all the joys were . . .

In the case of 'agreement noises' and short responses used in a sequence while someone else is speaking, we print these in brackets within the main speaker's continuous utterance at appropriate points, as follows:

A (yes) we don't have any bangers I can't stand those (yes) – just the . . .

Whenever what is on the tape is unintelligible, we use the convention ~~~ within the transcription. Words which are begun but unfinished are written out as far as they go, e.g. 'they are playi · playing'. Uninterpretable syllables are transcribed phonemically.

Extralinguistic effects, such as laughter, are printed in italics, as in A *laughs*.

Pause marking

Four lengths of pauses are marked, the shortest with a dot (·), the next longest with a dash (–), the next with two dashes (– –), and the longest with three (– – –). Hesitation noises, indicated by *er*, *erm*, *m* are transcribed in sequence with the text, as they occur. Hesitant *the* is transcribed *thi*. Observing the pauses, along with the intonation conventions below, will be sufficient to identify the sentences and other grammatical structures of the texts. Capital letters, which are purely features of the written language, are therefore unnecessary at the beginnings of sentences. We have retained them only in the case of proper names, to aid immediacy of comprehension, and in the case of the pronoun 'I'.

Intonation organization

The basic pronunciation units for connected speech are patterns of pitch movement which we call *tone-units*. A tone-unit is a distinctive configuration of pitches, with a clear centre, or *nucleus*. In our transcription, the thick vertical bar, |, indicates the boundary between tone-units. The nucleus is the syllable (or, in some cases, series of syllables) which carries the greatest prominence within the tone-unit. It has been given various names in the linguistic literature—'primary stress', 'primary accent', 'tonic syllable', for instance. It follows that the word—or words—which contains the nuclear syllable will correspondingly stand out as the most important word in the tone-unit, and this we print in small capitals. It is of major importance to get the placement of the nucleus right, as it is the main means whereby contrasts in emphasis are communicated in English, as in:

| he was a terribly NICE man| as opposed to
| he was a TERRIBLY nice man|.

General direction of pitch movement
The pitch movement on the nucleus is the main factor governing perception of the overall tune, and as contrasts here can condition considerable differences, the various nuclear movements are given some prominence in our transcription. Nuclei will be seen to fall (marked by ` over the vowel of the appropriate syllable in the word which contains it), rise (´), stay level (¯), fall and then rise (ᵛ), rise and then fall (ᴧ), and there are a few combinations of tones (e.g. fall plus rise, ` ´). The general movement of the rest of the tone-unit may be judged by observing whether a syllable involves a step-up in pitch, indicated by ↑, or a degree of stress only, indicated by '. Extra strong stress is marked by ". The only other important factor is that the first prominent syllable of the tone-unit, or *onset*, which identifies a speaker's average level of pitch, is marked by a thin vertical bar, |.

It should now be possible to follow the salient points of the transcriptions in relation to the main prosodic features as heard on the tape. For reference, however, we now give a complete glossary of all our symbols.

Table of prosodic features
| tone-unit boundary
| first prominent syllable of the tone-unit
`   falling tone
´   rising tone
¯   level tone
ᴧ   rising-falling tone
ᵛ   falling-rising tone
` ´ fall-plus-rise (on separate syllables)
'   the next syllable is stressed
↑   the next syllable is stressed and also steps up in pitch
"   extra strong stress

.
¯
_ _   } pauses, from brief to long
_ _ _

Further information about the kind of prosodic features and the system of marking them used here, and also details of features omitted from our transcription, may be found in Crystal (1969), Crystal and Davy (1969).

EXTRACT 1

Talking about football

*This extract was taken from a long conversation between
two men (B and C below), aged around 40, at the home of
one of the authors (A). All three participants had been
friends for years. The two men had been invited to have a
drink one evening—a regular event—and were unaware
that they were being recorded. (When told, afterwards,
it cost A many rounds of drinks!) The situation was very
relaxed. B, an accountant, is from Ireland, but has been
living in Berkshire for some years, and his accent displays
a mixture of the regional characteristics of both these
areas. C is a primary school teacher, who has also lived in
Berkshire for many years, but whose accent has remained
predominantly that of his county of origin, Yorkshire.
This passage comes from a point about an hour after
the start of the conversation. B has been complaining
about poor standards in sport and entertainment these
days. After an excursus about the cinema (see Extract 13),
A takes him up on why he thinks so poorly about football.*

A well |what's the · |what's the 'failure with the ↑FÒOTBALL| I
mean |this · |this I don't 'really ↑SÈE| I mean it · |cos the
↑MÒNEY| · |how 'much does it 'cost to get ÌN| |down the ↑RÒAD|
|NÒW|

B   I |think it ↑probably – it| 5
|probably 'is the ↑MÒNEY| for |what you ↑GÈT| you |KNÓW| – erm
I was |reading in the ↑paper this ↑MÒRNING| a a |CHÀP| he's a
DI|RÈCTOR| of a |big ↑CÒMPANY| in |BÌRMINGHAM| – who was th
the |world's ↑number 'one ↑FÒOTBALL 'fan| he |used to ↑SPÈND|
a|bout a 'thousand a ↑YÈAR| |watching FÒOTBALL| you |KNÓW| 10
(C: |CÒO|) – he's he's |watched 'football in ↑every n · on
↑every 'league · 'ground in ÉNGLAND| |all 'ninety TWÓ|
(A *laughs*) – and he's |been to A↑MÈRICA| to |watch ↑West
BRÒMWICH 'playing in A'merica| he's · he's |been to the la
to |ÒH| · the |LÀST| f f |two or 'three 'world CÙP| · |world   15
CÙP| · mat |THÍNGS| you |KNÓW| · |TÓURNAMENTS| – – and he |goes

to ↑all the 'matches AWÁY| you |KNÓW| |European ↑CÙP 'matches
and 'everything| that |ÈNGLISH teams are PLÁYING in| he's all
'over the ↑WÒRLD 'watching it yòu SÉE| – |THÌS YÉAR| he's
|watched ↑↑twenty 'two GÀMES| – |SÒ 'far| |this YÈAR| which is   2
a|bout · FÌFTY per 'cent| of his |NŎRMAL| (C: |good LÒRD|) · and
|even ↑HÈ's getting 'browned ↑ÓFF| and |HÈ was SÁYING| that
erm – you can |go to a NÍGHTCLUB| in |BÍRMINGHAM| – – and
|watch ↑Tony BÉNNET| · for a|bout ↑thirty ↑BŌB| – |something
like THÍS| a |night with ↑Tony ↑BÉNNET| – |have a 'nice ↑MÉAL| 2
· in · |very · ↑plushy SURRŌUNDINGS| very |WĀRM|
|NÍCE| |PLÈASANT| – says it |CÒSTS him| a|bout the ↑SÀME
a'mount of MÓNEY| to |go and ↑sit in a ↑breezy 'windy STÁND| –
(A & C *laugh*) on a · on a |WÒODEN BÉNCH| – to |WĂTCH a |rather
BÓRING 'game of ↑FÒOTBALL| with |no ↑PERSONÁLITY| and |all   3
DEFÉNSIVE| and |ÈVERYTHING| he |says it's just ↑KÌLLING itself|
you |KNÓW| (A: |YÈAH| C: |M̌|) – they're |not 'giving the
'enter'tainment they ÚSED to 'give| the erm – CON|DÌTIONS have|
if |ÀNYTHING| are |not are f DE|TĚRIORATED| and er (C: in |what
WÀY|) they're |charging f ↑three 'times what they ↑ÙSED to| ·   3.
or |four 'times what they ↑ÙSED to|

C in what |way have con'ditions DETÈRIORATED 'Gerry|
B well the |GRÒUNDS| are |scruffier than they ÚSED to be| I mean
  they |never DÒ these 'grounds ÚP| |DÒ they| I mean they're
  pro|gressively ↑getting ↑WÒRSE| 4(
C   you |KNÓW| I |thought they ↑"ÀLWAYS had these
  'wooden 'benches and STÁNDS and 'that|
B |YÈAH| but they've been |getting
↑WŎRSE| I |mean you ↑don't – er |every 'now and a'gain the
↑team 'builds a 'new STĂND| (C: |M̌|) · I mean the |stand that   4:
you ↑sit in on ↑most grounds ↑NŎW| is the |VÈRY 'same STÁND|
– you |sat in – ↑thirty ↑YÈARS ago| |forty ↑YÈARS ago| (C: |ÒH|
· |NÒW| |GÈRRY| i *coughs*) EX|CĚPTING| it's |probably
                        DE↑TÈRIORATED| ⁓

C   but there   50

|WÀS an 'interesti| you're |QUÌTE RÍGHT| there was |that one
that COLLÀPSED| (B: |YÈAH|) · but there |WÀS an 'interesting
'programme on these 'grounds| (B *clears throat*) the |way it
'showed 'talked a'bout the 'CONTINÈNTAL ones| |that one it |was
it in MADRÌD| · |they're ↑SUPÈRB| (B: |ÒH| |they're TREMÈNDOUS|)   55
· and the |way they could ↑CLĔAR them| in |x ↑number of
↑SÈCONDS| – a |crowd of s s erm ↑seventy THOÙSAND I THÍNK it
'was| |out of ÓNE 'ground| – they had · they had it s
|ÒRGANIZED| in |such a WÁY| that there was |so many ÉNTRANCES
'all round| – m |you KNÓW| · |ÀRCS| |like THÌS| |upstairs   60
DÓWNSTAIRS| – they're |all · FÙNNELLED in such| – I mean
they'd |all · pla · the PÀSSAGES| and |ĔXITS| |all ↑PLÀNNED|
in |such a ↑WĀY| that |everybody could ↑get ŌUT| you |KNŌW| –
and erm · it was |after that DIS↑ÀSTER you KNÓW|. (B:
|RÀNGERS| ⁓) I |think he 'said there was ↑only "one 'modern   65
GRÓUND in ↑ÈNGLAND| |RĔALLY| that could |CLÀIM to be MÓDERN|
|was it Man CÍTY| – – – (B: |CÓVENTRY 'maybe|) or |was theirs
'taken as 'one of the ÒLDEST| – but you |KNÓW| it |said – ↑ÀLL
ours| are |RÈALLY 'ancient| ex|cept · erm a'bout ↑one or TWÓ|
– com|pared with 'these 'CONTI↑NĔNTALS| – cos they're |all   70
↑built pu they're |purpose ↑BÙILT| – for |modern CON↑DÌTIONS|
· and |ours ↑ÀREN'T| · and |every 'time a dis'aster 'like
↑THÌS HÁPPENS| or |somebody 'gets ↑killed in a · or ↑trampled
in a ↑CRÙSH| – er a |STÁND 'breaks| · |this · erm – – |this
↑HĬGHLIGHTS it| and they sort of · |patch it ÙP| and it's   75
|BÒTCHED| you |KNÓW| thi · because · I sup|pose it's ALRÍGHT|
· |easy to TÁLK| but if |you've got · ↑so many 'thousand
'quid's worth of – ↑STÀND THÉRE| you're |not 'going to 'sort
of ↑knock it 'all DŎWN| and |build it from ↑SCRÀTCH| · you
just |patch it ↑ÙP| |DÒN'T you| (B: |YÈAH|) · of |CÒURSE| the   80
|CONTI↑NĔNTALS I sup'pose| they |came in ↑LĂTE| and they ·
|build them – (B: |PRÒPERLY|) you |KNÓW| this MI|LÀN 'ground|

· there's a |famous 'one ↑THÈRE ÍSN'T there| · (B: erm) you
|KNÓW| they were |saying ↑how SU↑PÈRB they 'were| · but the
|one in ↑SPÀIN| was the |BĔST| – (B: of |course) I |thought it   8
was in MADRÌD| – was it |Real MADRÌD| they were fan (B: they're
|all erm ⁓) oh they were FAN|TÀSTIC| it |showed the
↑PHÒTOGRAPHS 'of them| · |people ↑sitting 'there in the 'hot
SÚN| you |KNÓW| |smoking CI↑GĀRS| and · |out i and it |showed
the ↑crowds · ↑ÈMPTYING| – (B: |M̀|) they had a |practice – erm   9
↑ÈXIT| (B: |YÉAH|) – you |KNÓW| er – A|LÀRM · |ÒH| it was
FAN|TÀSTIC| the |speed that they got ↑ÒUT|

B oh |one 'minute there was · 'seventy THÒUSAND in the GRÓUND|
(C: |YÈAH| |YÈAH|) and about · |thirty 'seconds LÁTER| or a
|minute 'later they were ↑CLÈAR| 9

C   you |KNÓW| about · |ì don't KNÓW| about |twenty
↑ÈNTRANCES| (A: |YÈAH|) stra|tegically ↑PLÀCED| for |top and
↑BÒTTOM| you |KNÓW| |all ↑round the ↑GRÒUND| · (B: |YĒAH|) – you
|KNÓW| like |spokes from a ↑WHÈEL| they were |out in ↑NÒ time|

B   and   10
they |all 'went GÓ| |straight 'out of | out of the gr ·
com:|pletely AWÀY from the 'place| (C: |YÈAH| A: |M̀|) – – |ÒH|
|here in ↑ĔNGLAND| I mean you |all 'come ↑haring ÓUT| and
then you |all get 'into a f · a ↑FÙNNEL| – – a|bout er (A: |oh
↑YÈAH| a |JÀM|) a|bout as 'wide as · ↑two ⁓ 'two 'normal   10
↑DRÌVES I SUPPÓSE|

C |I went to
'Stamford ↑BRÌDGE last year ÓNCE| –

B |all ↑fifty 'thousand have
got to get ↑ÒUT through THÉRE| 11

C I'd |never ↑BÈEN BEFÓRE| · |CÒR| – |CÒR| the |CRÒWDS| · |ÒOH|
and you |WÒNDERED| if you were going to be |trampled to DÈATH|
they |started to SHÒVE| · do you |KNÓW| it's |quite
↑FRÌGHTENING| (A: |where was ↑THÌS TÓNY| B: |YÈAH|) |carrying
'Justin – |Stamford BRÌDGE| where I |went to see CHÈLSEA| 11

|play ↑LÈEDS| (A: |oh YĒS| |M̌|) – and |Leeds 'played
SHÒCKINGLY| – |worst 'game they ↑ever PLÀYED|

B well |some of the 'gates 'might be a'bout as WÍDE as ↑that
↑RÒOM| as the |RÒOM| |MÌGHTN'T they| |RĚALLY|

C |ÒOH| there were |KÌDS| 120
|sitting on 'that ↑great HÒARDING|

B a|bout as 'wide as THÁT| – and a|bout ↑thirty
↑THÒUSAND have to 'go out through ↑THÉRE| (C: |CÒR|) you |KNÓW|
I mean er (A: |M̌|) – oh it's |TÈRRIBLE|

C |ÒOH| the |sea of – ↑bodies in ↑front of you ↑MÒVING| and 125
|people 'started to PÙSH| BE|HÌND you| it got |quite
FRÌGHTENING| cos you |couldn't have 'done 'anything you'd have
been |absolutely ↑HÈLPLESS|

NOTES

3 *down the road:* i.e. at the football ground of the local team. The
ground was in fact about a mile away, and could not be approached
directly from A's house: this phrase is often used loosely and
colloquially to refer to a specific place in the vicinity of the speaker,
its identity being obvious from the context.

9 *number one* = chief, most important.

9–10 *he used . . . you know:* note the clear prosodic markers of parenthesis
here.

10 *thousand:* i.e. pounds.

12 *league ground: league* here refers to the formal association of clubs
for playing a particular game. The *Football League* in England has
92 clubs as participants. It is divided into four *divisions, first, second,
third* and *fourth*, these representing levels of football ability, as
determined by competition, the first division being top.

13 *West Bromwich:* short for West Bromwich Albion, at the time a
first division team, near to Birmingham.

15 *oh:* used here as a mark of hesitation preceding a definite statement.

16 *mat:* unfinished form of *matches.* B is searching for the right word
(*tournaments*) and not finding it very easily.

17 *away:* matches played by a team away from its home ground;
opposite: *at home.*

19 Note the prosodic contrast between the end of B's list of examples,
which use an increasingly lower pitch and reduced loudness, and
the beginning of his contrasting point, *this year . . .*

21 *normal* = norm, general habit. *Norm* is more usual than *normal,*
which as a noun tends to be restricted to specialist contexts. This is
probably an idiosyncrasy of B's.

22 *browned off* = bored, fed up.

24 *bob* = shillings (a coin now replaced by the 5 new pence piece). The conversation was recorded nearly a year after the introduction of the new currency in Britain, but the old system is still being referred to here (as it would be in other phrases expressing round values, e.g. *ten bob*).

24–6 Narrowed pitch range here marks B's use of Tony Bennet as a routine, illustrative case, one item on a potential list. Tony Bennet is not the only alternative to football in Birmingham.

26 *plushy* = luxurious, comfortable, especially in an artificial or pretentious way. The word comes from *plush*, a kind of velvety fabric, and usually occurs only in this colloquial sense.

26–7 Note this loose stringing together of adjectives standing for whole sentences. B is omitting a great deal of redundant sentence structure at this point, e.g. (*you can*) *have* (25), (*he*) *says* (27).

28 The effect of *breezy* is underlined by the held first consonants; likewise in 1.30, on *boring*.

30 *personality:* distinctiveness—either of individual players or of the quality of the game as a whole.

31 *defensive:* i.e. the players are always defending their own goal, and unwilling to attack.
   it's: i.e. the game of football.

37 *Gerry:* colloquial intimate form of *Gerard* or *Gerald*.

38 *scruffier* = more untidy, dirty, less cared for (generally colloquial)

39 *do . . . up* = renovate, repair, renew (colloquial)

45–6 Note the slow falling glissando pitch movement on the first part of this sentence, reinforcing a generally persuasive tone.

48 *excepting* = except that. Usually followed by a noun (= 'with the exception of'); as a conjunction, its use is archaic or regional.

51 *that one that collapsed:* C is referring to a recent disaster at a ground, when a stand collapsed killing a number of people. It is referred to again in 64, ff.

53 *programme:* C takes it for granted that the television is being referred to.

56 *x:* a colloquial expression of vagueness, which would be used only by someone conversant with mathematics involving variables. C cannot remember the exact number, but knows it was some definite figure. *n* is also used in this way.

59 *there was:* lack of concord typical of colloquial English.

60 *m:* more a belch than a hesitation. C's beer is beginning to affect his language a little at this point, as he tries to get a complex visual scene into words. His syntax becomes very disjointed, and his pronunciation a little slurred.
   like this: he is drawing the scene in the air.

61 *in such:* not a complete construction—he is anticipating *in such a way* (63).

64 see note on 51.

65 *Rangers:* Glasgow Rangers—a Scottish football team.

67 *Man City:* colloquial abbreviation for the first division football team, *Manchester City.*
   Coventry: another team in the first division.

67–8 Note the contrasting parenthesis: *was it Man* in a high pitch range; *or was . . . oldest* in a low range and with piano loudness.

71 *purpose built* = built to fulfil a particular need (as opposed to adapting some unsuitable building).

75 *highlights* = makes (it) stand out, underlines.

76 *botched* = mended in a temporary or clumsy way, patched up (also see 80); colloquial use.
   because construction is not continued; the following clause is a main clause.

77 *easy to talk:* in full, *it's easy to talk,* a common turn of phrase. Note the low pitch range and creaky voice at this point, indicating mild self-disparagement.

78 *quid:* colloquial for *pound.*

79 *from scratch* = from the very beginning, all over again.

81 *came in late:* i.e. began playing football relatively recently.

82 An instance of a common colloquial interaction, with C unable or not bothering to complete his sentence, and B supplying a word.

83 *isn't there:* B interprets this as a question (as one would expect from the rising tone on the tag), but C does not stop for an answer.

90 *emptying:* i.e. leaving the ground. Note the forceful glissando on this tone-unit.

101 *went go:* a substitution. B is unsure which tense to use: he is caught between C's past tense, and his own anticipated present tense.

103 *haring out* = running out wildly, i.e. 'like a hare'; colloquial.

104 *funnel* = narrow passageway.

105 *jam* = unmoving crush of people (due to narrow passageway).

106 *drives* = driveways (into houses).

108 *Stamford Bridge:* the home ground of first division team *Chelsea.*

111 *cor:* mild exclamation (originally a derivative of 'God'), expressive of almost any attitude, depending on context and intonation.

113 *shove* = push hard (generally colloquial).

115 *Justin:* C's child.

117 Note the husky tone of voice, indicative of disparagement.

120 *kids:* colloquial for *children.*

121 *hoarding:* either a screen of boards for displaying posters, etc., or a large wooden fence for enclosing an area. Either could be the sense intended in this context. Cf. 3.28.

125 *sea of bodies:* metaphorical expression for a large number of people entirely covering a given area.
   Note the colloquial syntactic order *in front of you moving* = 'moving in front of you'.

125–8 Note the extra prosodic features as C gets more involved in his story—wider pitch range, marked glissando movement, and increasing speed towards the end.

EXTRACT 2

Bonfire night

This extract is taken from a conversation between two women. A is in her mid-thirties, and has two small children while B is in her early twenties. Both speakers are now living in London —where the conversation took place— but they were born in different parts of the country, A in the Midlands, and B in Sussex. There is a slight Midlands accent still in A, mainly in her intonation. The two had not met each other before the evening of this conversation, with the result that they spent a good deal of time talking about each other's background and activities, and establishing areas of common interest. The situation was relaxed and friendly. At this point in the conversation, the speakers had already been talking for about half-an-hour, and were clearly getting on very well. They had just finished a lengthy and lively discussion about the merits of living in various parts of the country, and they are now looking for a fresh topic. There is a long pause, and then A introduces Bonfire Night. It is however done in a rather self-conscious way, and the conversation takes a couple of sentences before it gathers momentum. At times, it is obvious that they are simply keeping the conversation going (e.g. 20, 24, 34) in the absence of a topic comparable in interest to the one they had just finished talking about. The discussion is friendly, but polite and fairly restrained.

The recording was made at the end of October, and in view of the fact that A had children, it was not at all surprising that the conversation should have moved around sooner or later to the subject of Bonfire Night, which takes place on November 5th. As one of the few widely and enthusiastically observed English national customs, it is surprising how little is known about it outside England. Any foreigner in the country at the beginning of November, however, will be unable to make much sense of people's behaviour unless he is familiar with at least the following facts. Bonfire Night is also referred to as Guy Fawkes' Night. Guy Fawkes was one of a group who planned to blow up the King and Parliament, when they assembled in November 1605, by placing barrels of gunpowder in a cellar beneath the parliament building. The affair, known as the 'Gunpowder Plot', is remembered both ceremonially, in the annual search of the cellars beneath the Houses of Parliament, and individually, in the tradition of lighting bonfires and letting off fireworks on the evening of November 5th. The name 'Guy Fawkes' has given us the term 'guy' for an effigy intended to represent the plotter, which is burned on the bonfire.

In the weeks before November 5th, children may be seen with home-made guys on the streets, asking for money, ostensibly to buy fireworks. Their usual cry is 'Penny for the guy'. The custom of burning the guy is less common in these humanitarian days! Also, the law against selling fireworks to any child under the age of fourteen is being more strongly enforced, as a result of growing public concern about the high rate of accidents on bonfire night. The practice of having a bonfire, however, continues to be extremely widespread.

A we're |looking 'forward to ↑BÒNFIRE night| at |LÈAST| the
|CHÌLDREN ÁRE| – – do you IN|DÙLGE in 'this| –

B oh in · in |SÙSSEX we DÍD| – – I've – in |FÀCT| I |went to 'one
'last WÈEK| · but it was ·

A ⌇⌇ |that was a bit ÉARLY |WÁSN'T it|

B |all the |all the JÒYS were |JÒY| was
|taken ↑ÒUT of it for MÉ| be'cause it was – a ↑"HÙGE| |BÒNFIRE|
in a |garden the 'size of this ↑RŎOM| – with |big HÒUSES| |all
ARÒUND| – and the |bonfire was ↑right ÙNDER| a |big TRÈE| with
its |leaves ÁLL DRỲ| 1

A |M̄|

B and |I was ↑so WÒRRIED| · the the · |FLÀMES| were going |right
'up to the · 'lower 'branches of the ↑TRÈE| and | I was ↑so
WŌRRIED| about · |everything 'catching ↑FÍRE| that · |didn't
↑really en↑joy the ↑FLÀMES very ↑MÚCH| *laughs*   1.

A |NÒ| – I |don't think we can m 'manage a a 'large – ↑BŎNFIRE|
but the |FÌREWORKS| THEM|SÈLVES| – er we |have a 'little STÓRE
of|

B |oh YÉS| |THÈY'RE quite 'fun| |YÈS|

A |M̂| – – |yes the ↑CHÌLDREN like them| |VÈRY much| so – I   20
|think as 'long as 'one is ↑CÀREFUL| – |VÈRY careful| (|ÒH
yes|) it's all |RÍGHT|

B |M̄|

A – – but erm – – I I · I |ban all BÁNGERS| · we |don't have any
BÁNGERS| (|YÈS|) I |can't stand THÒSE| (|YÈS|) – |just the   2
PRÈTTY 'ones| – –

B |sparklers are my ↑FÀVOURITES|

A |M̄| |CÀTHERINE 'wheels are "MÝ favourites| |ÁCTUALLY| but er
– – t you |know we have ↑anything that's ↑pretty and SPÀRKLY|
· and |we have a ↑couple of "RÒCKETS| you |KNÓW| · to |satisfy   30
– – JÓNATHAN| who's |all – – RÓCKETS| and – SPÁCECRAFTS| and
|things like THÌS| –

B |M̄| – –

A so |that's FRÌDAY 'night| they |can't wait for THÀT| – – and
|keep ↑saying ↑well ↑couldn't we ↑"JÙST have 'one| · |just NŌW| 35
you |SĒE| *laughs (laughs)* · |trying to ↑use them ↑up be↑fore
the ↑actual ↑NĪGHT| –

B |YÈS| –

A t but the · |"Ī don't know 'where we can ↑get any ↑WÒOD from|
a|part from ↑chopping 'down a ↑few TRÈES| which I |wouldn't   40
'like to DÒ| – we |don't seem to 'have very much ↑WÒOD|

B |YÈS| |THÀT's a PÓINT| · |YÈS| – – |M̌| ·

A well I sup|pose if we 'went 'into the PÀRK| we |might col'lect
a 'few STÌCKS| but it's |not 'quite 'like 'having · "LÓGS| |ìs
it| – – but I |don't know 'where 'one would ↑GÈT 'this 'from   45
HÉRE| – – I er if |we were m · at "HÒME| · |back in the
MÌDLANDS| we would |KNÒW| if · you |KNÓW| |where we could GŌ|
and |GÈT all 'these things 'from| but

B |YÈS| |YÈS| · |M̄| – |M̄| · |in ↑SÙSSEX| – in |my VÌLLAGE|
they – |spent the ↑whole of · of · OC↑TÒBER 'building up the   50
BÓNFIRE| –

A |M̌|

B yes they |probably 'did it in ↑YÒURS|

A |they had a ↑VÌLLAGE one DÍD they|

B |YÈS| 55

A |YÈS|

B |YÈS|

A |YÈAH|

B |ÀLL the 'local 'people| – |HÉLPED with it| |put all their 'old
'ARMCHÁIRS and things| |ÓN it| 60

A |M̌| – |M̄HM| ·

B |used to be about ↑twenty feet ↑HÌGH | ·

A |M̄|

NOTES

The usual pronunciation of the name 'Guy Fawkes' Night' is /ˌgaɪ
'fɔːks ˌnaɪt/, but sometimes the version /'gaɪ ˌfɔːks ˌnaɪt/ is heard. Less
commonly, one may hear 'Guy Fawkes' on its own, as in 'Are you looking
forward to Guy Fawkes?' The word 'guy' can also be applied to any effigy
ceremoniously burned (e.g. 'They burned a guy of the Prime Minister').
·Note that in colloquial American English and increasingly in Britain,
'guy' is the normal form for 'man' or 'person' (as in 'This guy came up to
me and said . . .', 'What are you guys doing tonight?').

1 *at least* = at any rate.
Note the relatively low, quiet, and narrowed pitch range of A's
utterance, reflecting the rather awkward start to this topic. It contrasts sharply with 4, ff., as B takes the topic up more enthusiastically, but returns again at many points in the extract, e.g. 17–18,
21–3, 31–3.

2 *the children:* i.e. A's two children.
indulge = take part. An unexpected lexical item in this context,
used here to produce a slightly self-conscious, humorous effect.
The main sense of 'indulge' is 'gratify a taste or desire for' something (e.g. 'He indulges in ice-cream on Sundays', 'She's always
indulging herself'). There is usually an implication of luxurious
living or of permitting unrestrained pleasure. Since celebrating
Bonfire Night hardly falls into these categories, 'indulge' is in-
congruous in this context.

3 *in Sussex:* where B used to live.
one: i.e. a bonfire celebration. One may hear, for instance, 'I'm
going to a bonfire (night) at the Smiths' this evening'.

5 *a bit early:* as already mentioned, the recording was made in October.

8 *size of this room:* it is a fairly small room—in other words, emphasizing how dangerous the bonfire seemed in such a small
garden.

9 *big:* the held initial consonant adds extra emphasis to an already
emphatic passage.

10 *all* = very (colloquial intensifying use; cf. 6.60).

14 *that didn't:* the subject pronoun may simply be inaudible, or it may
have been intentionally omitted; it is abnormal to see this happening in a subordinate clause (cf. the more acceptable elisions in
35, 59). (See further, p. 104.)

16 *no:* the high narrow fall indicates that this is to be taken as an
agreement signal. It does not mean a contradiction. (See further,
p. 101.)

17 A emphasizes the noun phrase by putting it first. This gives an
unusual word order, as the hesitation indicates.
store: a nicely descriptive word, with its overtones of husbandry and
careful saving in a private place; cf. 'Squirrels storing their nuts'.

20 *so:* here to be taken with the following sentence. A is saying something like 'The children like fireworks. So I think it's alright to have
them, if one is careful'. The exact meaning of 'so' here is difficult to

define precisely: it implies that the speaker feels justified in making her next statement because of the truth of what she has just said, and might roughly be glossed as 'for that reason', or 'as a result'. The attachment of 'so' to the preceding sentence by intonational means illustrates a common process in slow-moving parts of conversations, where a construction that is to follow is anticipated, but its completion delayed. Cf. 'I like them because—they'll be so useful', where the pre-pausal conjunction indicates that the speakēr has not yet finished, and allows him time for thought.

21 Note the rhythmic form of the first tone-unit, as A expresses some feeling about the matter.

24 *bangers:* fireworks which (as one might expect) bang when they have finished burning. The pronunciation /ˈbæŋgəz/ is common in many accents of the Midlands and North of England, as opposed to R.P. /ˈbæŋəz/. It affects word-final /ŋ/ when this is made inter-vocalic due to the addition of a suffix, e.g. *singing* /ˈsɪŋgɪŋ/, R.P. /ˈsɪŋɪŋ/. Note that single-morpheme items in R.P. with medial /ŋ/ also have a pronunciation with /-g/, as in *finger*, *dangle*, etc.

27 *sparklers:* a kind of firework that may safely be held in the hand, or burned indoors, consisting of a piece of wire coated with a chemical which throws off brilliant sparks as it burns down. They are particularly popular with small children—and this may account for B's slight giggle at this point.

28 *catherine wheels:* a firework shaped like a wheel, which is attached by a nail through its centre to some suitable object; it then spins rapidly as it burns. (Also spelt *catharine* . . .) The name comes from St. Catherine of Alexandria, a 3rd century Christian martyr, who was tortured on a spiked wheel. The term 'pinwheel' is also used, especially in the USA.

29 *t:* this represents a click, a mannerism of A's, of no linguistic significance; also in 39.
sparkly: a nonce-formation (see p. 115) used here to define anything which gives off sparks, or 'sparkles'.

30 *couple* = a few. Not usually literally 'two', in colloquial speech. (Compare 10.86).
rockets: the fireworks—as opposed to 31, where the reference is to space rockets, as the context makes clear.

31 *Jonathan:* one of A's children.
all: a common colloquial use of *all*, which means 'completely involved in' or 'fully characterized by'. Note that 'all' in this sense is used only once in any list, before the first item. Another example would be: 'I never see John these days; it's all conferences, luncheons, and parties with him now'.
spacecrafts: note the unexpected use of *-s* here, influenced by the regular plurals of nouns in English. The normal plural is *spacecraft*.

34 *Friday night:* i.e. November 5th. As in 1, *night* here means 'evening'. It is quite common in this sense, e.g. 'That was a lovely night out' (said, for instance, upon one's return home just before midnight), 'Thank you for coming to our ladies' night'.

39ff   A lives in a built-up area of London, where there is little loose wood
suitable for burning in bonfires.

43–4   Breathy articulation here probably indicates A is getting bored with
this topic. The slow and precise articulation of 45–6 also indicates
this: with no good ideas available for keeping the conversation
going, A tries to contribute to the informal atmosphere by playing
with pronunciation.

44   *logs:* sections of tree-trunk.

47   *the Midlands:* a reference to the central part of England, where A
was born.

50–1   *building up the bonfire:* preparing the pile of loose wood, etc which
is to be burned on Bonfire Night. This is a practice which used to
keep children busy for several weeks before Bonfire Night, and it is
still common in areas where there are sufficient materials and space.
It is less common now in cities, where new building and landscape
development have left little unused open ground.

55ff   Multiple expression of agreement is a common feature of informal
conversation.

EXTRACT 3

News reporting

*The participants in this section are both men in their early
thirties. They each took an honours degree in English at
the same time and at the same University, where they
knew each other well; but after graduating, they had not
met again until this conversation was recorded—a period
of several years. Since leaving University, both have spent
their time teaching English; but whereas A has taught
mainly literature in English grammar schools, B has been
concerned with teaching English language to non-English
students in Cyprus. Partly because of this background,
but also because they are very interested in drama, both
having done some acting, they are extremely fluent
speakers, who introduce considerable dramatic effect into
their speech, and manipulate prosodic contrasts with
great subtlety. The occasion of the recording was at the
house of one of the authors, where they had been invited
for an evening. They had been left to talk on their own,
and the present extract comes from a point well in to their
conversation, in which both had been enthusiastically
participating.*

A er |two or 'three ↑YĚARS ago of 'course| we were |in the
↑thick of 'what was · called ↑PÀKI 'bashing| · did you |GÉT

that in 'Cyprus| did you |HÉAR a'bout it|

B |NÒ| well there are ⁓ |well I ↑yes I RĔAD

a'bout it| (|heard a'bout) in the |NÈWSPAPERS| in |English   5

↑NÈWSPAPERS| you |KNÓW|

A   you |just ↑HÈARD a'bout it| I |knew you 'wouldn't

↑GĒT 'that|

B |NÒ|

A |YÈS| 10

B |YÈS|

A but er – – th |that was A↑NÒTHER 'thing| where |NÈWSPAPERS|

were |absolutely IN↑FÙRIATING| – be|cause · I RE↑MĒMBER| ·

we'd |been on HÒLIDAY| we'd |taken a 'school 'trip to ÌTALY|

– – and – – |"SKÌNHEADS| had been |PÀRT of 'East HÁM| (|YÈS|)   15

you |KNÓW| for (|YÈS|) | for oh · |couple of ↑YÈARS| – and it

was · BE|GÌNNING to 'die 'out| – erm |PÀKI 'bashing| (*laughs*)

was – |at its ↑HÈIGHT| |THÉN| I SUP|PÓSE| erm · as |far as the

↑SCHÒOL GÓES| and as |far as ↑their sort of SO↑CÌETY 'goes| –

and |yet it was a ↑JÒKE| · it |wasn't a 'thing that they   20

'actually ↑DÌD| it was · |they 'rather 'liked the ↑WÒRD| it

was a |bit 'like (|M̀HM|) 'Cockney ↑RHỲMING 'slang| (|YÈS|) you

|KNÓW| (|YÈS|) *laughs* it sort of |had a 'nice ↑RÌNG to it| ·

|and they 'tended to get 'on quite ↑WÈLL| with the |PAKI↑STÀNIS

in 'fact| · |but ↑on the 'way BÀCK| – – – I remember for the   25

|first TÌME| |seeing · I |think it was a ↑SÙNDAY| or

|something like THÁT| or at |ÀNY 'rate| there were |Sunday

'newspaper ↑HÒARDINGS 'up| (|M̀|) – and it had |got an ÀRTICLE|

a|bout ↑SKÌNHEADS| in |one of the SÙNDAYS| –

B well I |must have ↑RÈAD that 'article ÁCTUALLY| |YÈS| 30

A   you |probably DÌD| · |and

it was the ↑first 'time the 'papers had 'cottoned ÒN to it| ·

and you |KNÓW| you could |see the ↑situ'ation DETÈRIORATE| ·

B |M̀|

A IM|MÈDIATELY| · there be|came – ↑very STRÒNG| |cliques of ·   35

↑SKÌNHEADS| and it be|came · 'UN↑CÒMFORTABLE| to |walk a'round
the 'streets of 'East HÀM| at |NÌGHT| – – and |PÀKI 'bashing|
· be|came a RE↑ÀLITY| · er you |KNÓW| a |very ↑VÌCIOUS 'thing|
(|M̌|) · there were |real · ↑CLÀSHES| · be|tween · the 'Pakis
and the ↑SKÌNHEADS| – – and and |that was 'almost EN↑TÌRELY   4(
pub'licity| you could |see it ↑CÒMING| I mean as |soon as I
'saw the ↑HÒARDING| · my |heart SÀNK| · be|cause 'skinheads
(|M̌|) had been 'with us a 'couple of ↑YĔARS| and |NŎBODY| had
|thought anything A↑BÒUT it| it was just |boys who went 'round
with short ↑HÀIR| · |rather 'like · you KNÓW| · |teddy 'boys   4:
in the 'mid ↑FÌFTIES| |went 'round with ↑LÒNG · 'hair| (|M̌|)
– – |but – as ↑soon as this ↑HÀPPENED| – (I sup|pose 'they)
you could |see 'what was 'going to HÀPPEN|
B the |press 'probably 'took 'one or 'two CĂSES| (|M̌|) and
ex|aggerated them ↑out of ↑all PRO↑PÒRTION| 5(
A |that's RÍGHT| – and it be|came a ↑FÀSHION|
B   ⏦ – |M̌| ·
A it was |HÒRRIBLE|
B   I'm I'm |very sus'picious of the PRÉSS| |GÈNERALLY|
and I can |TÈLL you| be|cause · |not 'only I |mean 'that's   5:
'that's ÒNE 'case| that you've |GÌVEN| (|YÈS|) but |ÀLSO| |in
in their RE↑PÒRTING| of erm af|fairs ↑foreign AF↑FÀIRS| –
A |YÈS|
B be|cause · ↑LÌVING in 'Cyprus| I've |seen · ↑quite a 'number
of HISTÓRICAL E↑VÈNTS| you |KNÓW| (|M̌|) I was I was |THÉRE| 6(
|when they · 'tried to as'sassinate MA↑KÀRIOS for ex'ample| –
A |YÈS| · |YÈS| of |CÒURSE| –
B and erm · |so 'much of 'this is ↑"blown 'up out of 'all
PRO↑"PÒRTION in the PRÉSS| – and · I |think it's DÀNGEROUS|
|partly for the 'reason that ↑YÒU'VE 'said| that · erm |in a   6:
WÀY| it |makes 'people BE↑LÌEVE| that a |situ'ation is 'very
SĔRIOUS| if they |read it in · er in ↑PRÌNT| you |KNÓW| in
|black and ↑WHÌTE| · (|YÈAH|) · th th th that it it |ìs

SÉRIOUS| – but |ĂLSO| · erm it's |just MIS'REPRESEN↑TÀTION|
be|cause · erm ↑ÒBVIOUSLY I mean| |when there 'wa 'was this   70
AS'SASSINÀTION ATTÉMPT| – erm |there ↑was – 'some TÈNSION in
'Cyprus| it would be |CHĬLDISH| to |say there ↑WÀSN'T| – but
|people 'went 'on 'living 'quite ↑NŎRMALLY| · and er it |wasn't
RÈALLY 'such a 'serious MÁTTER| I mean |FÓRTUNATELY| he |WÀSN'T
SHÓT | and |that was ↑THÀT| (|M̀|) you |SÉE| (|YÈS|) I mean w   75
|that's how 'most 'pe 'people ↑TÒOK it| (|YÈS| · |YÈS|) and erm
|so many ↑ÒTHER 'cases| as |WÈLL| |where there've 'been · erm
↑inter'national 'SITUĂTIONS| that erm – |people re · have
↑really just ↑taken as 'part of their 'normal LĬFE| and it
|"hasn't AF↑"FÈCTED| the |everyday ↑LÌFE of CÝPRUS| at |ÀLL| ·   80
A |NÒ|
B you |KNÓW| · and |yet erm · ↑when my ↑MÒTHER was ALÍVE| – |she
used to · erm be ↑so WÒRRIED| because erm she would |read in
the in the ↑PÀPER you 'know| |HÈADLINES| · er |crisis in
↑CÝPRUS and 'so on| and |she 'thought I was ↑going to be ·   85
'blown ↑ÙP| or |SHÒT or 'something| (|YÈS| · |that's RÍGHT| ·
|YÈS|) and there was |no er |no POSSI↑BÌLITY| of |any such
↑THÌNG| be|cause erm · it ↑may have af'fected a ↑small 'group
of ↑PÈOPLE| · but it was |largely a PO↑LÌTICAL 'issue|
A |M̀| 90
B and the |thing is that the · er ↑JŎURNALISTS| I mean I've |MÈT
'some of 'these 'people| – they know |"NÒTHING a'bout the
CÓUNTRY| at |ÀLL| they · they |go to the · 'Ledra 'Palace
HOTÈL for EXÁMPLE| and they |sit at the BĂR| – and they
ab|sorb you know 'one or two FÀCTS| from a |few PÈOPLE| but   95
|they 'don't 'know the ↑LĀNGUAGE| and they |don't 'know the
↑PĒOPLE| and they |don't · ↑really 'know the 'SITU↑ÀTION| –
they're |not FÌT| to · to RE|PÒRT these things| in er in
|such ↑DÈTAIL| · and |yet they ↑DŎ you 'see| – –
A well I I – it AN|NÒYS me no 'end reading NÉWSPAPERS| – |really   100
DÒES| I |get ↑so ÌRRITATED| with |almost ÊVERYTHING| – |if you

↑start to 'read them – ↑reasonably SÈRIOUSLY| – er you |start
to 'see ↑all the · the ↑FLÀWS| in |what they're ↑SÀYING| and
· |if you've had an EX↑PÈRIENCE| or |you've been 'on the
↑SPÒT| – – and |seen the ↑DÌFFERENCE| between the re|ality and   10
what's RE↑PÒRTED| (|Ḿ|) you can I|MÀGINE what it is|

B |YÈS| – well |there you ↑ÀRE you 'see| |that's it

A   ⁓ · and |how the 'whole 'thing 'blows ÙP| |rather
like · have |you you've |read SCÒOP · HÁVE you| .

B |NÒ| 11

A |Evelyn WĂUGH| be|cause it's (|NÒ|) – ↑just LÌKE THÁT| er it's
|very ↑CLÈVER ÁCTUALLY| it's |one of · 'Evelyn 'Waugh's ↑BÈST
I THÍNK| – be|cause he's ↑got this – er ↑situ'ation where a
↑MÀN| is |going 'off to re'port on 'some – 'trouble 'somewhere
in A↑MĔRICA| · I've for|gotten the 'details NÓW| – but he   11
|gets 'on the 'wrong TRÀIN| and |ends 'up in the 'wrong PLÀCE|
– – and |finds that he's ↑in a PLÁCE| that's |perfectly QUĬET|
and |perfectly ÍNNOCENT| and there's |no ↑STÒRY| – and |so he
'just ↑WRÌTES 'one| – and with|in a ↑WĔEK| he's |managed to
cre'ate ↑RÌOTS| you |KNÓW| the |whole 'place is 'in a FU↑RÒRE| 12
both laugh er th – i |it can ↑HÀPPEN| · you |KNÓW| you can
|SĔE 'these things| (|YÈS|) I mean (|YÈS|) that's |obviously
'taking it to EX↑TRÈMES| but – they've got TRE|MÈNDOUS 'power
'like ↑THÁT| and |I think it's ↑FRÌGHTENING|

B well they |HÀVE| 12

NOTES

1 The extract commences with a change of topic. A marks this with a
   marked jump in pitch at the beginning of *two or three years ago*, and
   reinforces the effect by speaking the whole phrase slightly more
   slowly than his norm.
2 *in the thick of* = in the middle of, involved most in.
   Paki: the colloquial and originally offensive abbreviation for
   Pakistani, i.e. an immigrant to Britain from that part of the world.
   (*Pak* is another widely-used abbreviation, though not in this col-
   location, with *bashing* (= beating).) The whole phrase refers to the

beating-up of immigrants by gangs, which was common for a short time in the mid-1960s. The point is developed in 35, ff.

get: A means (as he goes on to say) 'receive information about', but B responds to the other interpretation of 'happen, take place' before A has time to clarify. The confusion takes a few lines to sort itself out.

2–3 *did . . . Cyprus:* this is a good example of the way in which high pitch and reduced loudness can be used to make a question sound interested.

12 *another:* this refers back to a part of the conversation before this extract.

12–13 A pronounces *newspapers* more quietly and with slight breathiness to show how strongly he feels about what he is saying. The same features are also heard on *absolutely*, but here the effect is made even stronger by the high pitch jump on the first syllable, and the delayed release of the /b/.

14 *school trip:* an excursion by a party of schoolchildren.

15 *and:* emphatic drawl here marks a significant stage in the development of the narrative.

skinheads: gangs of youths, common in the 1960s, whose distinctive feature was very closely cropped hair. Increased loudness and tension show that this is a key word in the conversation.

East Ham: a suburb of East London.

16 *it:* i.e. the skinhead fashion and mentality.

16–17 *and it was beginning to die out:* the high pitch, increased tension and very much delayed release of /b/ introduce a kind of 'cautionary' note, which warns B that care is needed in interpreting the phrase. (As we see a little later on (37), Paki-bashing did not in fact die out.)

18–19 *as far as . . . goes:* note the way in which this idiom retains its present tense form, even in a past narrative context where one might expect the use of a past tense.

18–20 A is qualifying his statement that Paki-bashing was at its height: the low pitch and reduced loudness from *then* to *goes* suggests that this is additional and less important information. The end of the addition is shown by a return to normal pitch and loudness, plus an increase in speed, on *and yet . . .*

19 *school:* i.e. the school where A worked.

their: i.e. the schoolchildren's.

21 The precise pronunciation of *did* emphasizes that the verb is being used in its lexical meaning.

22 *Cockney* = London (used as an adjective here).

rhyming slang: a conventional rhetorical pattern, traditional in certain kinds of London speech, in which a word is replaced by the first part of a phrase that rhymes with it, e.g. *He stood on my plates* = *He stood on my feet* (because *plates* is short for 'plates of meat', which rhymes with *feet*).

23 *ring* = appealing quality—in this case, of the sound.

24–5 A introduces a note of mock surprise by means of the very high pitch from *and* to *Pakistanis:* the effect is to suggest that B is being

told the opposite of what he might have expected to hear. A dramatic contrast is then introduced immediately, through the precise *but*,
and the height, tension and quietness of *on the way back*, indicating
that A is about to introduce an important new part of the topic.

28 *hoarding:* a large board carrying advertisements—in this case for
advertising the Sunday newspapers. (American English: *billboard.*)
A's construction could mean that 'special hoardings are erected for
Sunday papers', but this does not happen, and so he must be using
the word here to refer to the advertisements themselves. This kind
of transference of sense ('metonymy') is quite common in English
(e.g. when *the crown* comes to stand for the monarchy).

29 *Sundays:* conventional colloquial abbreviation for 'Sunday newspapers'.

31–3 *and it was . . . deteriorate:* note the increased force given to this by
gradual reduction in loudness.

32 *cottoned on to* = realized, taken notice of (colloquial).

35 *cliques* = exclusive groups (a word which is usually pejorative in
force).

35–6 *very strong . . . skinheads:* more emphasis, but this time by means of
glissando pitch movement.
became = emerged, developed (not a common use of this verb).

38 *vicious:* marked lip-rounding on the first syllable adds considerable
emotional feeling to the sense of this word.

40–5 A passage in which there is detailed and complex use ^f many
fluctuations of pitch, loudness, and especially speed, as A gives an
emphatic reformulation of what he has been saying.

45 *teddy boys:* youths of the 1950s whose hair and clothes were in the
style of the time of King Edward VII.

46 *mid fifties* = the middle years of the decade 1950–60.

47 *as soon . . . happened:* note the reduced loudness for contrast.

57 *affairs:* the first occurrence of this word is rapidly supplemented by
the more explicit gloss *foreign affairs* —so rapidly that the rhythm
of the tone-unit is not disturbed at all.

60–1 *I was . . . Makarios:* the low, monotone pitch signals a parenthesis
and at the same time gives the impression that B is trying not to
sound too dramatic.

63 *blown up* = exaggerated. Also in 108.

63–4 B is using a very wide pitch range, plus a number of strongly
stressed syllables, to show emphatic disapproval. He does so again
in numerous places in the rest of this extract.

68 As B's stammer suggests, he has lost the thread of the complex
correlative construction begun in 65 (*partly for . . .*). The reason for
his difficulty is that he has tried to make the *if*-clause in 67 depen-
dent on two clauses at once, one preceding and one following, viz.
(a) *People believe that a situation is very serious if . . . white.*
(b) *People believe that   if . . . white, it is*
                                                                          serious.

84–5 *crisis in Cyprus:* this imaginary headline is given increased rhythmi-
cality as a means of showing that it is a 'quotation'.

95 *absorb:* a nice choice of word, blending the senses of 'taking in through the ears' and 'taking in through the mouth'.

95-7 *but . . . situation:* B uses the narrowed pitch range and level nuclei which are typically associated with a list in English. He is also using them in this instance to convey his feelings of scorn, and the rhythmic parallelism he introduces into the list gives it rhetorical force. The fact that his disgust has reached its peak is signalled by the extremely high pitch of *they're not fit.*

100 *no end:* = very much. A colloquial and very emphatic phrase, usually found in the construction '*it* + *Verb* + *Pronoun* + *no end*'. (Cf. also its use in such phrases as *there was no end of a quarrel* = 'there was a very great quarrel'.)
really: note the colloquial omission of the subject.

100-2 A's rather quiet resumption of the previously vigorous conversation in a low, narrow pitch range shows how strongly he agrees with the feelings just expressed by B.

101 *irritated with almost:* the laugh that can be heard here is continued as a smile, and the effects of this on A's articulation may be heard on *everything* and the next few words. A is perhaps amused by the strength with which he is expressing himself (100-1).

103 *flaws:* mistakes, fallacies.

104-5 *on the spot:* i.e. present while some event took place. The precise pronunciation of this phrase, as also of *experience,* suggests that A is using these phrases as if they were quotations.

112 *Evelyn Waugh:* 'by' is here understood.

114-5 A realizes that he has begun to give details that are not really necessary for the point he is making: by adopting a low pitch from *some* to *now,* he reduces the importance of what he is saying, and this anticipates the contrast which comes with his resumption of normal level (115).

120 *furore:* an alternative pronunciation to /fjuːˈrɔː/ is /fjuːˈrɔːri/.

123 *they:* i.e. the reporters and the newspapers.

123-4 *they've got . . . frightening:* very wide pitch range and reduced loudness for emphasis.

EXTRACT 4

Pigs

This extract is taken from the very end of a half-hour conversation between two women in their thirties (A and B), with their respective husbands (C and D), also in their thirties, just having entered the room. A and C are from Liverpool, B and D are from the Midlands, and though all have lived in the South of England for some years, they display degrees of regional pronunciation. A and B are housewives, but B also does some primary-school teaching (referred to in line 40). C and D are university teachers. The occasion is that the two couples, who have known each other for a number of years, have been brought together, the wives not having seen each other for some time. They have been catching up on each other's news, and at this point in the conversation A has been telling B about her family's summer holiday, when they went to stay on a farm. Her young children had been particularly impressed with the animals—especially the pigs.

A oh and |one 'pig DÌED| be|cause it ÀTE too 'much| (B: |ooh
RÉALLY|) |ÒH| it was RE|VÒLTING| |oh they were ↑TÈRRIBLE| the
|PÌGS| (C: oh ∼) they made a |dreadful ↑row in the ↑MÒRNING|
when it was |FÈEDING 'time| – and |ÒNE PÍG| it was erm · a
|YÒUNG 'pig| a|bout · THÀT 'size| you |KNÓW| m |MÌDDLING| –
|and erm – it was ↑DÈAD| and it was |LÝING 'there| I'd |never
SÈEN a 'dead 'pig BEFÓRE| |absolutely STÌFF|

B   di the |children SÀW it DÍD 'they|

A |oh they were ENGRÔSSED| you |KNŌW| (C: |oh YÈS| ∼ it was
|MÂRVELLOUS|) erm they |thought this was ↑WÒNDERFUL| · |and
erm · they ∼ they 'asked 'why it was DÈAD| – and er · the
|farmer · ap↑parently · ↑didn't 'want his ↑wife to KNŌW|
be|cause · he'd ↑over'fed them BEFÔRE| · and she'd been
|"FÙRIOUS| – and of |course he was ↑trying to 'keep it FRÒM
her| but |all the KÎDS| were a|gog a'bout this 'dead ↑PÌG|
and ∼ was |telling them 'not to 'tell the 'farmer's WÍFE|
(D: |YÉAH|) and |all THÌS| – so this |pig was ↑absolutely DÈAD|
so they · |put it on · they |have a 'sort of 'smouldering
HÈAP| that |smoulders all the ↑TÌME| so they |went to ↑burn
the ↑PÌG| – and |all the ↑KÌDS| | ∼ *laughs* (C *laughs*) –
|hanging 'over the ↑GÀTE| |watching this ↑PÌG| ∼ |and they
were ↑very er ↑very 'taken that the ↑pig had ↑DÌED| be|cause it had
ÈATEN too 'much| you |KNŌW|

D |what a 'marvellous DÈATH|

B |a MŎRAL in ↑that ↑SÒMEWHERE| 25
C *laughs* but |didn't 'one 'pig 'eat AN↑ÒTHER 'pig|
A |YÈS| (B: ⁓) ⁓ |that was be↑fore we were THÉRE| · er|oh
   NÒ| |YÈS| |one of the ↑mothers (C: yes |that's ↑really ↑CRÙDE|
   |ÌSN'T it|) |YÈS| it |had · ↑PÌGLETS| (D: they'll |eat ÂNYTHING|
   ⁓) and it |ate 'all the LÌTTER up| 30
B |oh the – they'll |eat ÀNYTHING he 'says| *laughs*
A |ÒH 'yes| ·
   |YÈS|
D |YÈS| · |TÝPEWRITERS| – |BÁBIES| (B: well |YÈS| |QUÌTE|) |dead
   CÁTS| · |CÓAL| 35
A |YÉS| |oh YÈS| be|cause the |when they ↑FÈD the 'pigs|
   they |all had to ↑stand 'well ↑BÀCK| and they were al|lowed to
   'take the ↑BÙCKETS| but they |weren't al'lowed to get NÈAR the
   'pigs| –
B |ÀH| · well · |we ↑took a |we 'took some 'children on a ↑VÌSIT| 40
   to er · |Enfield's en↑viron↑mental · ↑STÙDY 'centre| · the
   |other DÁY| · and |they have 'various 'animals a'round THÉRE|
   |one of · WHÍCH| is a |PÌG – er |PÌNKY| · |PÌNKY| |that's
   RÍGHT| · and |all the CHÍLDREN| (C *laughs*) |stood 'round the
   'OUTSÍDE| – – (C: |M̄|) |like THÍS| at the |FÉNCE you 'see| and   45
   |this 'large 'slobbering PÍG| (A *laughs* |YÈAH|) was al|lowed
   ÓUT| · |into the MÚD| – (C *laughs*) and |each 'child was ↑given
   a 'slice of ↑CÀRROT| you |SÉE| (A: |oh ↑NÒ|) and |they · ↑poked
   it THRÓUGH| – and er |this PÍG| |twice a DÁY| you |SÉE| cos
   |they had ↑two VÍSITS| a |DÁY| (A & B *laugh*) so |twice a DÁY| 50
   |this 'pig was FÉD| |by ↑twenty – 'slices of ↑CÁRROTS| *laughs*
   (*All laugh*) and |Pinky 'looked a VÈRY 'happy 'pig| (D *laughs*)
A |these
   'pigs ↑VÀRIED| be|cause ↑SÒME of the 'pigs| |they y you could
   |sort of ↑just 'walk ↑THRÒUGH them| but |ÒTHER 'pigs| (B: |M̄|)   55
   you |couldn't go ↑NÈAR| be|cause they'd ↑BÌTE you| and |ÈAT
   you| (C: |M̄|) and |THÌS 'sort of 'thing| ⁓

C they were |horrible ↑filthy ↑SNÒRTING 'things| |WÈREN'T they|
  (A: |oh they ↑WÈRE| ⁓)

B |they ÀRE re'volting| |ÀREN'T they|
  al|though a ↑friend of ÒURS| who · w was |so · ↑passionately
  ↑FÒND of PÍGS| that – |he 'came · (D: ⁓) |he 'came
  from NÒRFOLK| you |SÉE| and he |came to the er ↑MÏDLANDS| – er
  to |TÉACH| and he I |think he was ↑very SÀD| for the · the |lost
  'fields of ↑NÒRFOLK or SÓMETHING (A: |Ṁ |) be|cause when↑ever
  we were ÓUT| he would |stop the CÁR| if |ever he 'saw · 'or
  SMÉLT| |sign of a PÍG| · the |car STÒPPED| it |didn't 'matter
  ↑WHÈRE it WÁS| and he |went 'out ↑looking for the PÌGS| – and
  would |lean 'over and ↑TÀLK to them| |FÒNDLY| |WÒULDN'T he|

D |YĔAH|

B these |DÎRTY| · |SHÙFFLING| |MÒNSTERS| in – |ÀCRES of 'mud|

D |YÈS| he was |really
  AFFÈCTED by 'pigs| ·

B |yes he WÀS| I could |never come to TÈRMS with THÍS| ⁓

C |sounds a 'bit ↑STRÁNGE|

NOTES

1 *oh and:* A has suddenly remembered a further point about the pigs.
2 *revolting* = disgusting, repugnant.
2–3 Glissando pitch movement is very expressive of A's intense feelings
   here. It occurs at various places during this extract.
   they were terrible, the pigs: construction typical of colloquial speech.
5 *that size:* A is using her hands to show the size.
   middling = middle or average size.
9 *engrossed* = fascinated, absorbed.
15 *agog about* = very excited about, eagerly interested in.
17 *so* = anyway (cf. 18, where *so* = therefore).
19 *heap:* i.e. of rubbish.
20 *kids* = children (colloquial).
   ⁓: A makes an expressive noise and puts on a facial expression,
   imitating the mixture of trepidation and delight the children were
   showing.
21 *hanging over* = leaning well over.

28 *crude* = ill-mannered, rude. C is referring to the eating of the pig in 26.

38 *buckets:* i.e. the buckets of pig swill.

41 *Enfield:* a suburb of north London.
Note that B pronounces the noun phrase *Enfield's environmental study centre* with a mock refined accent, perhaps because she feels she has introduced a note of academic formality into the conversation.

43 *Pinky:* a traditional name for a pig (cf. *Fido* /'faɪdəu/ for dogs, *Polly* for parrots),

46-7 An expressive description, with tempo variation playing the main part in producing the effect (note especially the clipped syllable in *mud*).

48 *oh no:* the intonation here shows that the sense intended is an expression of humorous sympathy with the point of view expressed: it is not a contradiction.

49 *cos:* usual colloquial abbreviation for 'because'.

50 *they:* i.e. the animals.

53 *these:* i.e. the ones in A's story.

61 The *who* construction stays incomplete, and the sentence continues with the verb *was*. The same thing happens in 62: the *that* construction stops, and *he came* starts a new clause.

63 *Norfolk:* a country area in the east of England.

67 *sign:* no article audible. It is possible, though not usual, for the article to be omitted in such a context in colloquial speech.

71 *shuffling* = moving the feet irregularly and without lifting them clear of the ground.
acre: a measure of land, 4840 square yards—i.e. approximately 4000 square metres. B is of course exaggerating. (Cf. p. 114).

73 *affected* = emotionally moved.

74 *come to terms with* = learn to live with, accept.

75 *sounds a bit strange:* i.e. it sounds as if the man has something (mentally) wrong with him.

EXTRACT 5

A driving incident

This story is taken from a leisurely conversation between two friends, one afternoon when both were on holiday. A is from the Midlands, and B from Lancashire, but both have worked in the south of England, in Universities, for several years. The topic up to this point had been entirely connected with cars, and the unexpected things that can go wrong with them. B has just told a horror story from his own experience, and A responds with one of his own favourites. There is no hurry, and so A, having obtained B's full attention, tells the story in a very controlled style, with prosodic effects dramatically introduced and descriptive details added to regulate the pace of the narrative.

A |yes I RE↑MÈMBER| there was a |TÊRRIBLE| |STÔRY| – |HÔRRIFYING 'story| that was |told by a ↑CÒLLEAGUE of MÍNE| when |I used to TÈACH| |YÈARS AGÓ| – |who erm · |this 'chap 'lived in erm – a ↑semi deta · de'tached HÓUSE| and |next DÓOR| – there was · a |MÁN| who'd |just 'bought a 'new CÀR| – and |he was TÈLLING me| that |one MÓRNING| he was |looking 'through the WÍNDOW| – and |this · MÁN| al|lowed his ↑WÎFE to 'drive the 'car| |very UNWÌSELY| and |she was 'having a 'first GÒ in it| – (|M̃|) · and – |he BÀCKED it| |ÒUT of the GÁRAGE| – |so that it was ↑standing 'on the ↑DRÌVEWAY| · and he'd |closed the 'garage DÓORS| – (|YÉAH|) · and – |she 'came ↑out of the HÓUSE| – to · |take this CÀR out| and |go ↑SHÔPPING for the 'first 'time| – so she |CÀME out| |very GÌNGERLY| – and |opened the DŌOR| · and |sat in the CĀR| – and – er · be|gan to BĀCK| · |very very GÈNTLY| – |taking · ↑GRÉAT CÀRE you 'see| that she |didn't do ↑ÀNYTHING to this · to this 'new 'car| – and – – |as she BÁCKED| – there was an |un'pleasant · ↑CRÙNCHING 'sound| (*laughs*) and she |SLÀPPED on the BRÁKES| and |looked a'round FRĀNTICALLY| – and |RĚALIZED| that she |hadn't 'opened the · ↑GĂTES| · that · |let on to the 'main ↑RÒAD you 'see| (|ÒH|) · and she'd |just ↑BÀCKED into 'these| |"very GÉNTLY| and (|M̄|) sort of |touched the BÚMPER| and |bent the GÀTES 'slightly| (|M̄|) – and |this put her 'into a 'bit of a FLÀP| · (|M̄|) so – be|fore she could do 'anything A↑BÒUT THÍS| she |had to 'pull ↑FÒRWARD| (|M̄|) · in |order to er to ↑ÒPEN the GÁTES| – |so she – ↑took the 'car ↑out of REVÉRSE| · |put it 'into · 'first GÉAR| (|YÈAH|) and |pulled 'forward ↑very ↑GÈNTLY| (|YÈAH|) – but – UN|FÒRTUNATELY| . she · |mis'judged the ↑distance to the ↑garage DÓORS| · so that |as

she 'pulled FÒRWARD| · she |RÂN into the 'garage DÓORS| ·   30
|THÙMP| (*laughs*) and |smashed 'in the ↑front ↑BÙMPER of the
CÁR| · and (|ÒH|) |bent the 'garage ↑DÒORS| (|YÈAH|) – so she
|STÒPPED in 'time| · you |SÉE| – and by |THÌS STÁGE| she was
|getting 'into a ↑bit of a FLŪTTER| · (*laughs*) so · she got
|out of the CÁR| (*laughs*) |shaking 'like a LÉAF| – |went ·   35
BE↑HÌND the CÁR| and |opened the 'gates · that ↑let on to the
'main RŎAD| (YÈAH|) and |then she · was de↑termined 'not to
be DE↑FÈATED 'by this 'state of AFFÁIRS| which was |pretty
TÉRRIFYING| |GÔT into the CÁR| – and – – |"started the ÉNGINE| ·
· |"looked 'through the 'back WÍNDOW| |very 'very CÀREFULLY| ·   40
and · backed ÓUT| with the |utmost DELIBERÀTION| · |into the
'main RÓAD| · and |managed it ↑absolutely ↑PÈRFECTLY| – but
the |only 'trouble WĂS| · that · she'd |left the DRÎVING 'side
'door| |ÒPEN| · and had for|gotten to CLÓSE it| · so that |as
she 'backed ÓUT| |through the GÁTES| |into the 'main RÓAD| she   45
|tore 'off the ↑DŌOR| (*laughs*) – – AP|PÀRENTLY| at |WHÌCH STÁGE|
she |just COL↑LÀPSED| and |went into a ↑state of HYS↑TÈRIA|
B *laughs* |ÒH 'God| · I |thought you were going to 'say she was
going to ↑hit the ↑MÌLKMAN or something|
A |no NÔ| 50
B |HM̀| – t |oh BLÌMEY|

NOTES

1 A begins rapidly, indicating his intention to take the lead in the
conversation at this point.
Colloquial omission of the indefinite article before *horrifying* (cf.
4:67).
2 *colleague:* a formal term to refer to one's co-workers in a given job;
particularly used by members of the various professions.
3 The *who* clause would have referred to the 'colleague', whereas A's
story is about someone else—hence the change of construction.
4 *semi-detached* = a dwelling containing two houses joined by a
single shared wall.
5 As A gets into his story, his speed increases, and his tone units
become shorter and even in length.

8 *very unwisely:* male teachers are advised not to dwell on the implications of this adverbial in front of classes of female students!

10 *driveway* = the approach to a house within its grounds. Less common than *drive*.

11 B produces a breathy laugh, anticipating the kind of thing likely to happen in the story. (A's own smile can be heard through some of the spread vowels at this point.) Later on, B's laughter becomes more overt. Without these reinforcing utterances, A would not feel that his story was being appreciated.

13 *gingerly* = warily and gently.

14–15 Note the rhythmical, level tone sequence, with increased tempo, as A approaches the climax of the first part of the story.

18 *crunching:* the *cr* is lengthened, adding an onomatopoeic effect to the story at this point.
slapped on the brakes: emphatic colloquial expression, meaning 'braked', with the implication of sudden contact, Cf. 8.70.
Note the increase in A's speed here, as he reaches an exciting point in the narrative.

20 *let on* = led on, opened on. Also in 36.

21 B's utterance, in a low husky voice, indicates the interpretation 'I don't believe it!'

24 *flap* = fluster, panic.

25 *pull* = drive the car.

30 Note the piano level as A approaches the climax of this part of the story.

32 *bent the garage doors:* regional (Midlands) intonation pattern (and to a lesser extent, vowel quality) here—also below (46) on *tore off the door.*

34 *flutter* = nervous state, panic, flap (cf. 24).

40 There are many dramatic narrative effects in the prosody here: in particular, one should note the glissando, breathy quality of *very very carefully*, and the high tense articulation of *utmost deliberation.*

43 The structure is [*driving side*] *door*.

48 *oh God:* the lax, drawled quality is important in order to produce the jocular effect.

51 *t* = the alveolar click, usually written *tut*, and here expressive of B's sympathetic appreciation, both of A's story and the predicament reported in it.
blimey: mild exclamation, here expressing a mixture of emotions—surprise, disbelief, sympathy, in particular.

EXTRACT 6

Living in London

Shortly before this conversation was recorded, the speakers had both graduated in English from London

*University, where they were fairly close friends. B is in
her early twenties, and A is a little older. The extract is
taken from the middle of a conversation when they were
left alone after supper at the home of one of the authors.
While at University, both had lived at their homes in the
suburbs of London, but B had recently moved to a flat
much closer to the centre of the city, and the extract is
largely about her reactions to this move. It begins with A
concluding a story about her own home town (the* it *of the
first line), for which she had little liking.*

A |ÒH| it was the most un|friendly un↑pleasant 'place you could
   'wish to ↑KNÒW| –

B well it *laughs* |SÒUNDS a 'bit 'like| |where ↑WÈ'RE 'living 'in
   a WÁY| |not · |not like · ↑that en · EN↑TÌRELY| but – what I
   · |what SUR↑PRÍSED me| was |when I 'came 'down to YÓU| I   5
   |THŌUGHT| well – you re|member what ↑SHÈANA 'said| a|bout the
   ↑TRÈES| and the ET|CÈTERA| (the |TRÈES| |YÈS| the) I |THÒUGHT|
   my |last 'sight of the ↑CÒUNTRY| (the |trees *laughs*) you |KNÓW|
   – |as I · ↑came 'back to LÒNDON| · and er – |THÈN I DISCÓVERED|
   |how · how |lovely 'Maida Vale ↑ìs| (it's a |BEAÙTIFUL 'area| 10
   · |M̌|) |I can ↑see TRÈES| from my |WÍNDOW| – and · |walking ·
   |walking to ↑SǍINSBURY'S| is |LÒVELY| because there's there's
   · there's some |"FLÀTS| and there there's |lots of LÀWN| · and
   then |TRÈES| and · some |lovely ↑ÒLD 'houses| on the |other
   'side of the RÒAD| and – it |really · |in the ↑AÙTUMN I 'mean| 15
   the |LĚAVES and 'everything| (|YÈS|) it |looks ↑really ↑LÒVELY|
   and it's a |very WÌDE 'road| |TÒO| there are |WÌDE 'roads
   'everywhere 'there| it's |not 'like – ↑where we 'lived in
   ↑London BEFÓRE| · |it was ↑DÌRTIER| and |SMÒKIER| I |MÈAN| it's
   |very DÌRTY in 'Maida VÁLE| (|M̌|) |Ì'VE 'noticed THÁT| I |mean   20
   · erm · ↑just from the ↑point of 'view of ↑CÙRTAINS| and ·
   |looking at the 'dirt that 'comes 'onto the WÌNDOWS| and er
   – – AL|THÒUGH| er the ha |MỲ 'window| |opens 'onto a ↑SÌDE
   RÓAD| – erm the the |DÌRT| is TRE|MÈNDOUS| and my |HǍIR 'seems
   to 'need 'washing| |twice as ↑ÒFTEN| and (|M̌|) |ÈVERYTHING   25

'seems| to |get DÍRTY| – but erm – – it's |just · RÂTHER nice|
in the |sense tha't · ↑WHÈRE – the 'mews ÍS| erm – – |on – – |on the
way 'up to ↑KÌLBURN| – you've |got · m · well it's · it's |more
of a · er · a ↑CHÈAPER| it's |not a SE↑LÈCT 'shopping 'centre|
by |ÀNY 'means| |and there're 'lots of · CÓUNCIL 'houses| and
|FLÁTS| and – erm – |I 'mean I |I 'think it's dil it's
FAN↑↑TÀSTIC| be|cause you can ↑GÒ 'up 'there| and they're |very
'nice ↑LÒOKING – FLÁTS and 'everything| it's I · it's |been
FÀIRLY 'well DE↑SÍGNED| · and you can |go ÙP 'there| and and
|shop ↑RÈASONABLY| – but · |at the ↑same TÌME| |just 'where
WÈ'RE 'living| |there's a ↑sort of ↑SPRÌNKLING| of of |little
DELICATÈSSEN| and ex|travagant and ex↑traordinarily ex↑pensive
↑SHÒPS| (laughs) you |SÉE| and |very ex'pensive ↑"CLÈANERS
ETCÉTERA| – and |"I've Leen 'doing ↑little SÙRVEYS| of the
|ĂREA| and and |LÒOKING| you |KNÓW| and you can – |find sp
'things ↑ÈQUALLY 'good| in |other SHÔPS| erm · and ⁓ the
|SÈRVICE| is |equally GÒOD| but you j you can |just 'pay ↑twice
as MÙCH| ac|cording to 'where you GÒ| – erm · and |THÈN| · |in
the ↑ÒTHER DIRÉCTION| |up to St John's WÒOD| it's sort of
|just · the wa · |one RÒAD| that |RÙNS| |by the ↑side laughs
of er – ↑our ↑HÒUSE| · er |leads ↑straight 'down to the – |WÈLL|
|right into the 'heart of Little VÈNICE| |which is ↑BÈAUTIFUL|
– i I |MÈAN| in I |hadn't RĔALIZED| how |absolutely 'lovely it
↑ÌS|

A   is · |Little 'Venice
where the CA↑NÀL ÉNDS|
B |YÈS|
A   laughs it |SÒUNDS as though it DÍD|
B |so the CA↑NÀL 'runs| at the |end of
'our ↑RÒAD| it |takes er it's A|BÒUT| – – – |WÈLL| · a |LÈISURELY
'walk| in |ten MÌNUTES| you're |down b a|long 'by the CA↑NÀL|
– and |TH ÀT of 'course| is the |NÌCEST part| there's some
|lovely ↑HÒUSES| |but it's the ↑TRÈES| you can |stand on the

↑BRĬDGE| – and |look · |look ALÒNG| and the |trees at the
↑MÒMENT| |oh it's ↑BEAÙTIFUL| |all GÒLD| in the |WÀTER and   60
'everything| |I MÈAN| |one 'gets 'quite POÈTIC ABÓUT it|
but – – |on a ↑SÙNDAY| when er · |Sundays in ↑LÒNDON| · |if
you're |if we're ↑all WÒRKING| or |CÒOKING| or |things
like THÀT| it can get |FÈARFULLY| |DÙLL| – and er · to |go
'out for a 'walk THÈRE| it's it's |just BEAÙTIFUL| – |"SÒ| ·   65
|what is ↑NÌCE THÓUGH| |is the is that we're ↑in a ↑nice
COSMO↑PÒLITAN 'little 'area| – I |MÈAN| the there |ÌSN'T the
'snobbery of| of EX|ÀCTLY| – erm – you |KNÒW| |east and WÈST|
or (|M̃|) |going · a DI|VÌDING| |LÌNE| or |anything 'like THÀT|
but er – you've you've |got 'all 'these 'lovely HÒUSES| 70
et|cetera ET↑CÈTERA| · erm · which i I I · I'm |GLÀD| that
you've |got these ↑ÒTHER| sort of |FÛNNY 'little 'places|
and |FÛNNY 'little 'shops| and · erm – – you |KNÓW| m |ÒLD
'London|

NOTES

1 The quiet tone of this sentence helps to suggest that A has finished
what she wants to say. Note also the drawl on *unfriendly*, and the
falling glissando pitches throughout, which emphasize A's pejorative attitude towards her home town.

3–4 *in a way* = in some respects.

6 *Sheana:* a (rather uncommon) girl's name.

7 *etcetera:* a favourite phrase of B's, which she uses when she does not
feel it necessary to list all the details of a description. Cf. more usual
phrases, such as 'and the like', 'and so on', 'and things'.

10 *Maida Vale:* a mainly residential area approximately two miles
north-west of the centre of London. Note the way in which the
sudden diminuendo on this clause makes it stand out as a fresh and
serious point, contrasting with the more boisterous and jocular
opening of B's utterance.

12 *Sainsbury's:* the name of a leading chain of supermarkets. Using the
proper noun where one might expect a common noun (e.g. 'walking
to the supermarket') strikes a humorous note—the implication is
that life is built around this particular supermarket.
lovely: the initial consonant is drawled, adding intensity to the
utterance at this point. B uses this prosodic device a lot (along with

other variations in tempo, breathiness, and wide pitch range), e.g. *wide* (17), *from* (21), *fantastic* (32), and throughout line 37.

13 *flats:* British usage; cf. American 'apartments'.
lawn: a stretch of closely cut grass, especially in gardens or in front of buildings.

16 *the leaves:* B pronounces *the* with a slurred [d] and an [i] vowel—an abnormal articulation, for which there is no obvious reason.

17 *there are:* note the extent of the elision.

19 *I mean:* should be taken along with the following construction—i.e. Maida Vale is dirty as well.

21 *the point of view of curtains* = as far as the business of keeping the curtains clean is concerned.

27 *mews:* originally a collection of stables, usually built on either side of a narrow yard. Many of these have now been converted into living areas.

28 *Kilburn:* an area of London north of Maida Vale.

28–31 Note the low narrowed articulation, indicative of parenthesis. Also in 40–3.

29 *select* = discriminating, socially exclusive—and thus probably more expensive!

30 *council houses:* houses built by the local government authority ('the council') and let out to tenants.

31 *think:* unexpected pronunciation of *th-* [dθ], perhaps because B changed her mind about what to say at the last moment.

32 *fantastic:* general-purpose term of emphatic approval, much in vogue in the late sixties, especially among young people, and still quite popular. Note the extra intensity added by the drawled initial consonant.

32–4 The creaky vocal effect at this point indicates a mildly disparaging viewpoint on B's part, reinforcing the falling-rising tones.

33 *and everything:* i.e. and everything else about them.

34 *you can:* note the extent of the elision.

35 *reasonably:* i.e. there's a reasonable selection of goods at reasonable prices. Note the tense [iː] vowel, which accompanies a hesitant or doubtful expression on B's face: she is not particularly confident about how reasonable the shopping is.

36 *sprinkling of . . . shops:* an expressive phrase in which B is exaggerating somewhat—and is aware of doing so. The rhetorical balance of the phrase is marked by the alliteration, the rhythmic falling glissando pitches, the drawled consonants (ex*t*ravagant, ex*t*raordinarily, ex*p*ensive, sho*p*s), the slower pace of the whole phrase, and the gradual increase in loudness.

37 *delicatessen:* a shop selling various kinds of food, such as different types of cooked meats, cheeses and preserves, especially the more unusual and imported kinds. B avoids the plural 'delicatessens', which would most often be used here, possibly because she is aware that she is already using the plural form of a borrowed German word, *delikatesse*, meaning 'delicacy'.

38 *cleaners:* i.e. of clothing.

42 *just:* used loosely as an intensifier.

43 *according to where you go:* i.e. if you are not careful, and do not look around first, you may end up paying twice as much. *according to* = depending on.

43–4 *in the other . . . :* The slower tempo indicates a change of direction in the narrative. Cf. again at 62.

44 *St. John's Wood:* another residential area close to Maida Vale.

45 *laughs:* B is amused by the way A was absent-mindedly rubbing her hand on the arm of the chair in which she was sitting.

47 *Little Venice:* this is a part of London close to Maida Vale where the Regents Canal (referred to in 51) joins the Grand Union Canal in what is known as a 'canal basin'. The collection of waterways and boats which use them was thought to be reminiscent of Venice, though on a much smaller scale—hence the name.
beautiful: piano loudness and breathiness identify B's emotional bias here.

50 *is:* unexpected pronunciation [iš].

55 *well:* the low pitch, creaky voice and drawl on this word combine to produce a 'meditative' interpretation.

57 *there's:* note the lack of concord, common in informal conversation.

60 *all* = quite (colloquial intensifying use; cf. 2.10).
gold: i.e. their reflection adds a golden tint to the water.

61 *one:* rather self-conscious at this point—B switches to the more formal pronoun.

63 *working:* i.e. doing work at home—in the case of B and her flatmates, academic work.

64 *fearfully:* an intensifying adverb, with a general meaning; B might have used 'awfully', 'terribly', 'frightfully', 'jolly', and others, with very little difference.

65 *so:* a summarizing use, indicating that B has come to the end of her discourse on that topic—though she still adds a further point!

67 *cosmopolitan* = composed of many types of people—especially people of different nationalities, and especially with no sense of exclusiveness.

68 *east and west:* this refers to a point made by A earlier on in the conversation, who had been complaining of the way in which her home town had tended to split into two areas based on considerations of social class.

69 *going:* an unfinished construction; *or* links directly with *a dividing line*.

71 *etcetera etcetera:* in the sense of 'and things like that', *etcetera* may be used on its own, or repeated up to three times. It is rare to hear it repeated more frequently.

72 *funny* = intriguing, quaint.

73–4 *old London:* the articulation and syntax suggest a quotation. This is the kind of phrase you would expect to find in a travelogue or advertisement.

EXTRACT 7

Channel crossing

*The occasion is an informal supper party at the house of B
and C, who are husband and wife. A and D, also husband
and wife, have been invited over for the evening, and this is
part of the pre-supper conversation. A is from South
Wales, but has lived in England for many years; B and C
are from the north of England. The two couples have
been friends for several years, but have not got together
for a few months. The following extract occurs well into
the evening, during a passage where the two families have
been comparing holiday experiences. A and D have just
begun to talk about their holiday in Denmark, and about
some of the problems involved in choosing the best means
of crossing the English Channel.*

A but it was |LÒVELY| |ÒUR one| with the |NÍGHTCLUB| and we |had
a · we |had a ↑super CÀBIN| which was |just BE↑LÒW the
NÍGHT'CLUB| – – |"utterly SŎUNDPROOF| · you know |when you
'think what HÒUSES are LÍKE| · (B: |M̆|) · when we |shut our
'cabin DÓOR| · you |wouldn't 'know there was ↑ÀNYTHING OUTSÍDE|
and |yet there was a ↑NÍGHTCLUB| |pounding ↑MÙSIC a'way|
(C: |M̄|) · just |one – j im↑mediately 'OVERHÈAD| and |we were
the ↑cabin ↑next ↑TÒ it| *coughs* · (C: ⁓) and you |couldn't
HÈAR it| · at |ÀLL|
C |good HÈAVENS| 1
B   that's |GÓOD| |VÈRY 'good| ⁓
A |and it's of |CÒURSE| we could
|SÀY to the CHÍLDREN| we'll |just be UP↑STÀIRS| and |they
KNÉW| they |just had to k 'put (D: |M̄|) their ↑DRÈSSING 'gown
ÓN| and |come ÚP| (C: |YÈAH|) if they |WĂNTED us| · and |that   1
was ↑SÙPER| –
C w |were you · |did you have a ↑CĂR with you| ·
A |M̆|
D |M̆| · it's |all (C: |how) in↑cluded in the PRÌCE|

C I |SÈE| (A: |ÒH I ⁓) er · |how 'did you 'get – I mean |how   20
   did you 'find ↑THÀT 'side of it| be|cause · (A: |MÀRVELLOUS|)
   you |KNÓW| (D: ⁓) |some 'people 'say that that · (A: ⁓)
   'driving a ↑car a↑cross a ↑FÉRRY| is the |DÈVIL of a 'job| ·

D |ÉH|

A well |this was *clears throat*   25

D   a|cross a

C I |mean ↑taking a ↑car a↑cross – to the ↑CÒNTINENT| (A: |NÒ|) on
   on a |FÉRRY| (A: it's it's) is is |HÈLL|

A |NÒ| it |isn't at ↑ÀLL|

D |WHỲ| 30

C I |don't ↑KNÒW but ⁓

D   well I |mean we · we've · done it ↑nu I |mean
   the a|cross the ↑CHÄNNEL| – is |that what you MÉAN|

C yes that's wha (D: in|nu) EX|ÀCTLY what I 'mean| a|cross the
   ↑CHÀNNEL| 35

D   IN|NÙMERABLE 'times| there's |no there's |no there's |no
   (A: it's |NÓT|) TRÓUBLE with it| I don't

C w w – |WÈLL|

D |well you 'just drive the thing ÓN| you get |ÓUT of it| you
   |take what you WÁNT| (B: |Ḿ|) you |lock the CÁR up| · (A: |M̂|)   40
   |you |you · you |go to ⁓ if you |want if you've |got a
   ↑cabin ⁓ if it's a |NÌGHT| |THĬS 'crossing| you
   |AUTO↑MÀTICALLY had a 'cabin| · but · |on the |on the 'cross
   'channel ones you DÒN'T| – but if it's a |DÀY one| you can
   have a |DÀY 'cabin| (A: |M̂|) if you want to |PÀY for it| |only   45
   a ↑couple of ↑PŎUNDS| (C: |M̌|) · I mean it's |probably ↑WÒRTH
   it| with |KĬDS| · (C: |M̌|) and you just ⁓ (A: |WÈ always ·
   'did| |YÈS|) ⁓

C   well I'll |TÈLL you the 'sort of 'thing (A: |M̂|)
   I've HÉARD| I mean (A *coughs*) |ev |every SÙMMER| · er you   50
   you |see 'stories of tre↑mendous QUÈUES| at the

D   but |they're

'people who haven't ↑BÒOKED | –

A | YÈAH | – and | people (B: | M̌ |)

D | mind YÔU | | LÀST 'summer | there | was a 'WEEK↑ÈND when | (A *coughs*) · i · th the | queues were so BÂD | that | even 'people who'd ↑BÒOKED | couldn't | get to the ↑BÒATS |

B   and yeah it was | something to do with the ↑STRÌKE though | | WÁṢN'T it |

D | YÈAH | there | was (A: | YÈS |) there | was there | was 'some · some TRÓUBLE | as | WÈLL | | YÈS | | that's RÍGHT |

A but | CÈRTAINLY | (D: but | we've "NÊVER had | | ÀNY 'trouble) | in the ↑PÀST | (C: | M̌ |) | we've 'just ↑RÒLLED up | if we | go 'South'ampton le 'Havre or CHÈRBOURG | | then we BÒOK | – | and · I ↑do 'wonder ↑what would HĂPPEN | | if 'for ex'ample (D: we | haven't 'been the 'other 'way for a few ↑YÈARS |) there · there are | often 'people 'who · 'broke ↑DŌWN for ex'ample | so they | missed their BÒOKING | (C: | M̌ |) or their | CHĪLD has been 'ill | so they'd | STŌPPED 'somewhere | and they've | missed their BÓOKING | and | those 'people have to 'wait for a ↑VÀCANCY | (B: | YÈAH | C: | M̌ |) in the | years WÉ'VE been | they've · they've | got ↑ÒN ÚSUALLY | – there | haven't been MÀSSES of 'people 'waiting to 'get ÓN | · but – – | when · the | year that we ↑DÌD 'break DÓWN | we · were | actually ↑booked 'back a↑cross from Bou↑logne or (D: | CÀLAIS ⁓ |) ↑CÀLAIS or SÓMEWHERE | and | we 'just 'drove ↑ÚP | and got | on to the ↑BÒAT | that | happened to be ↑THÈRE |

D | YÈS | as it | HÀPPENED | that was a | very 'busy WEEK↑ÈND | and they | put on ↑lots of ↑extra ↑BÒATS | and | we ar'rived (A: | YÈS |) sort of 'late on a 'Saturday ↑ĔVENING | and we | just ↑drove ↑straight ↑ÒN |

C | WÈLL |

D and we were | very ↑LÙCKY |

NOTES

1 *it:* i.e. the boat
  it was lovely, our one: note the colloquial order.

7 *just one:* incomplete construction.

10 *good heavens:* polite, mildly emphatic exclamation.

12 *and its:* incomplete construction.

14 *gown:* the concord rules of colloquial English are much more flexible than in more formal varieties. Here, A obviously means *gowns* (one for each child), but the context is so clear that she does not bother to use the plural form.

21 *marvellous:* note the marked breathiness, expressive of A's emphatic conviction.

23 *devil of a:* mildly intensifying phrase, meaning 'terrible', 'awful'.
   job = task, problem.

24 *eh:* informal usage for 'pardon' (in the sense of 'please repeat'); considered ill-mannered in formal or respectful contexts—children, for example, are often told 'Don't say "eh", say "pardon"'.

28 *hell:* i.e. physical and mental torture.

32 ff. D is so surprised at C's attitude that his syntax becomes very disjointed as he tries to make a number of distinct points rapidly. New constructions begin after *nu* (32), the (33), *no* (twice, 36), *don't* (37), *to* (41), *want* (41), *cabin* (42), *night* (42).

38 *well:* a hesitant, doubtful intonation, C being rather taken aback by D's forceful reply.

39 *thing:* i.e. the car.

42 *this crossing:* i.e. on a special night-time crossing—as opposed to the general, everyday sailings, referred to in 43 simply as *the cross channel ones.*

45 *only:* subject and verb elided.

47 *kids:* children (colloquial).

53 *booked* = reserved a place in advance.

59 *strike:* there was a withdrawal of labour in support of a pay claim which caused many cross channel boats to be cancelled, with the result that long queues built up for a few boats which continued to operate.

61 *trouble:* i.e. special difficulty. (D is paraphrasing B's remark in 58–9.)

63 *rolled up* = arrived, turned up. A colloquial phrase, which can apply to people on foot as well as in vehicles.

64 *Southampton Le Havre:* i.e. from Southampton to Le Havre. It is normal in stating journeys to omit the prepositions: another example is 'I like the London Edinburgh journey in summer-time'.

66 *there:* A probably begins a new construction here, the *if*-clause staying uncompleted.

67 *broke down:* i.e. their car broke down en route to the ferry.

68 *or:* note the drawl here, indicating that A is listing examples randomly, and not seeing the alternatives as part of a fixed, closed list.

78 *as it happened* = in the event. A diminishing connecting phrase

(see p. 90); the subsequent context disallows the interpretation of
as = 'while' (i.e. 'while it was happening').

EXTRACT 8

Mice

*This extract is from earlier on in the same conversation as
that from which Extract 7 is taken. This time, A is in the
middle of a long explanation of how she came to have
mice all over her house. In the first part of her story, she
tells how her children had managed to bring some mice
home as pets, and she continues with some of the problems that then arose. As in Extract 5, the largely mono-
logue situation permits A to make great use of prosodic
contrasts in rhythm and speed.*

A so |ÀNYWAY| |all 'went WÉLL| · ex|cept that they were ↑very
BÔRED with the MÍCE| and |David 'kept on 'saying we 'ought to
'get ↑RĬD of them| so |ì said to JÓNATHAN| would you |like to
'play ↑CÌRCUSES with 'these MÍCE| – |out'side 'one 'after'noon
in the ↑SŬMMER| – |and we DÍD| and |one DEPĂRTED| – |having
been ↑let out 'into this 'grass A↑RĔNA| – and was |never 'seen
AGÁIN| · but the |other 'one CLÚNG| |very 'much to its CÁGE|
and |wouldn't 'go A↑WÀY| it |got 'out and went ↑BÀCK| – so
|this 'one was 'living 'on its ÓWN| – *coughs* |nobody · was ↑sad
a'bout the ↑other one being LÓST – and |then we went 'off to
↑DÈNMARK| – – |and – a↑bout · ↑ÒH| · at |LÊAST 'eight 'weeks| ·
|after 'we 'had – er w we · the · the ↑one had ES↑CĂPED| – – –
the |children 'cleaned out the CÁGE| · |under PRÓTEST| |as
ÚSUAL| and dis|covered there were n 'nine or e↑leven ↑"BÀBIES
in this 'thing| · (C *laughs*) |SÉE| (C *laughs*) im|maculate
CON↑CÈPTION| |ÒBVIOUSLY| (C: |Ḿ|) · |WÈLL| – we |calcu'lated
their ÁGE| (C: ⁓ it's |ha it's |happened BE↑FÒRE you KNÓW|
⁓) and we |MÌSCALCULATE| (D *laughs*) we |MÌSCALCULATED it|
|ÒBVIOUSLY| be|cause by the ↑time we · were ↑ready to 'give ·

they |found ↑HÒRDES of 'children| who |wanted – who |WÀNTED   20
these 'pets| so there was |no · |no ↑PRÒBLEM a'bout 'that| but
we |had to 'wait till they were ↑WÈANED| – and by the |time
'we 'reckoned they were ↑WÈANED| and we'd |done it on a
↑CĂLENDAR| |you KNÓW| and they |weren't 'quite ↑old e'nough to
↑mate with their ↑MŎTHER| · (B *laughs*) and we |tried to ↑CĂTCH   25
them| · (D: |or one A↑NŎTHER| C & D *talk*) |BLÒW 'me DÓWN| they
|cleaned 'out the CÁGE| · and there were A|NÒTHER 'nine|
B |ÒH 'lord|
A so ⁓ (B *talks to cat*) we were |reaching a 'stage of
HYS↑TÈRIA| (B *talks to cat*) well er |they – they were (B *talks*   30
to cat) 'sort of they |still looked 'very small ↑MÌCE 'this
'first 'litter| (B: |YÈAH|) · |and they 'seemed to have been
'crossed 'with a · with a 'KANGA↑RÒO| – be|cause they 'didn't
↑MÒVE| · |HORIZÓNTALLY| (D *laughs*) they |only ↑moved
↑VÈRTICALLY| *laughs* – and – |David 'kept 'saying 'something   35
'ought to be ↑done a'bout the MÍCE| – – and |everybody s 'kept
'saying well ↑ì 'can't DÓ it| · so |ÌN the ÉND| *clears throat*
when |Bridget 'had a ↑very · ↑very sort of ↑matter of 'fact
↑friend 'home to TÉA| (C *clears throat*) |she · 'and ↑BRÍDGET
and 'I| |shut 'our'selves in the ↑down'stairs LÒO| |having   40
↑emptied it of the ↑ĪRONING 'board| the |SWĒEPING| – the
|HŌOVER| the |PŌLISHER| – and |all the 'rest of the
'things ÍN it| – and |brought 'in 'this BÒX| – the the
                    |CÁGE| and a |BÓX| and a |BÚCKET|
D |which had been ↑kept in the 'garage   45
⁓ · for · |WHÀT| |two or 'three 'weeks be'fore ↑THÉN| ·
would it |be in the ↑GÁRAGE| · ⁓
A |I dis'covered that the ↑MŎTHER|
|who had been ↑THÈRE the 'day BEFÓRE| |wasn't ↑ÌN it| and |who
was ↑now ↑so BĪG| having |had ↑two LĬTTERS| that she |couldn't   50
· ↑easily ↑GÈT 'through the BÁRS| · just |wasn't ↑THÈRE| which
was |very ÓDD| |well we ↑caught · I |don't know ↑HÒW 'many of

these 'little 'mice| we |CÁUGHT| – there were |two 'we 'found
DÉAD| · |under'neath the ↑CÀGE| as |if they'd |somebody'd ·
↑picked 'up the 'cage and ↑DRÒPPED it 'on them| which was a
|bit ÓDD| – – but |ÀNYWAY| there were |MÀSSES of them| so |then
I · ↑put them 'all in this ↑plastic ↑BŬCKET| (D: ∼) it |took
a ↑took us ↑forty ↑MÌNUTES| to |CÀTCH them| and |all we 'had
to ↑DŎ| was to |get them 'out of this ↑CĀGE| and |into · the
↑bucket with the ↑LÌD 'on| · (C: |M̌|) · |but they were – |they
'just 'went 'like ↑THÌS| and they · |you'd go you know and
they'd ↑shoot 'out 'through the 'bars of the CÁGE| – and they'd
be |off and AWÀY| |little 'grey 'smooth (B: |ÙGH|) ↑SLÈEKY
'things| (C: |ÙGH| *laughs*) – and |we used |in the ÉND| we
de|vised a ↑very 'good ↑TRÀP| which was a |toilet · |TÒILET
'roll| · the · the |roll in the ↑MÌDDLE of it| – an |empty ·
↑TÒILET RÓLL| – *coughs* · and · |blocked 'up 'one SÍDE| · with
|TĬSSUES| and they as |soon as they 'saw THÍS| |they'd go
↑ÌNTO it| (B: |M̌|) – and |then ↑if you 'had 'found · ↑someone
'brave e'nough to ↑slap their 'hand on the 'other ÉND| ·
(C: |M̌|) · you could |empty it 'into this ↑BÙCKET| (C: |M̌|) – so
|then I 'put all 'that lot 'out in the ↑GÀRDEN| – |HOWÈVER|

B   they can |SWÌM| |CÀN'T they| |MÍCE|
D   you |put them 'out in the ↑GĂRDEN| –
A |YÈAH| well |what ÈLSE was I 'going to 'do with them|
D   I |thought you ↑flushed them ↑down the
↑LÀVATORY|
A   well |only the ↑DĔAD ones| and |that 'took so LÓNG| (C: |ÙGH|) I
wasn't |going to 'do the ↑LĬVE 'ones| (C: |down the LÁVATORY|)
B |mice ↑SWÌM
'though| |DÓN'T they| – |swim like ↑MÀD|
A   well |this one was ↑DÈAD| so it |wouldn't ↑swim very 'far ∼
B   I re|member my ↑BRÒTHER 'trying to 'drown a MÓUSE| ∼
A |ì 'reckon 'they WÓULD| |YÈS| I I I · I |reckon a MÓUSE| is
|capable of ↑ÀNYTHING| (B: ∼) |going to the ↑MÓON|

|ÀNYTHING| (B: |YÈAH|) so |ÀNYWAY|

D |I didn't 'realize you'd ↑let those
things ↑loose in the ↑GǍRDEN| no |"wonder we're in'fested by
MÍCE|

A |well they er it was a |very 'cold NÍGHT| and they'd |never   90
been 'out · BEFÓRE| and I thought (D: well they'd |been 'out
in the GǍRAGE| · which |wasn't particularly WÁRM|) and it was
|very DÀMP| and I |thought they'd ↑soon be DĒAD| of pneu|monia
if 'nothing ↑ÈLSE| – |HOWÈVER| · there was the |mother
'UNACCÓUNTED for| and |one who'd es'caped we'd ↑SÈEN 'go 'out| 95

D   ⁓ at |LÈAST ' one| at
|LÈAST 'one| ·

A |one · |I'm st · I'm |being FÀCTUAL DĀVID|

D   ⁓ well it |could have 'been – – |YÈS| well it |could
have 'been 'far ↑MÔRE| – be|cause there were   100

A |HOWÈVER| |we
'thought it's 'in the GĀRAGE| |so · |then ↑one 'Sunday MÓRNING|
|David ↑cleaned 'out the 'garage COM↑PLÈTELY| and they're
|TÈRRIBLY 'clever| |we 'had – to↑matoes in there RÍPENING| ·
|wrapped up in ↑NÈWSPAPER| · |each 'one 'indi↑vidually   105
↑WRÀPPED| – and · |"every 'one that was RÌPE| that had |really
TÚRNED| – the |mice had ↑ÈATEN| the m |mouse or MÍCE| had
|ÈATEN a 'little 'bit of| · and the |ones that HÁDN'T 'turned|
they |hadn't ↑TÒUCHED| (C: |M̆|) · you |KNÓW| they |hadn't even
↑nibbled at the ↑PÀPER| ·   110

C |CLÈVER|

NOTES

1 *so anyway:* a connecting phrase, used in a loose sense to indicate
that the narrative is about to take a completely fresh direction,
usually referring back to a point made earlier.
they: i.e. the children.

2 *David* and *Jonathan* (3): A's husband and child respectively.

5 *departed:* choosing this more formal verb (instead of *left*) attributes

more importance to the mice than one might expect, and an ironic effect is thereby introduced.

6 *arena:* an enclosed area in which some specific activity takes place. A is referring to the garden as if it were a circus arena.

11 *oh:* hesitant use preceding a specific quantity. Note the drawl, and the generally slower pace of the narrative at this point.

13 *under protest* = complaining (i.e. that they did not want the chore of having to clean out the cage).

14 Rising glissando pitches express the approach of a significant point in the development of the narrative. Cf. also 33.

15–16 *immaculate conception:* the phrase refers technically to the Roman Catholic dogma that the Virgin Mary was conceived without original sin; but in fact A is using the phrase ironically in the sense of the Virgin Birth—i.e. the mice appear to have been born without the aid of a mouse father!

17 *it:* i.e. an immaculate conception.

19 *because:* used here in a loose sense as a connecting word (cf. *so* in line 1); no specific sense of causality is intended, as can be seen from the subsequent context.
give: incomplete construction.

20 *hordes:* colloquial exaggeration for 'lots'.

22 *weaned:* able to survive without their mother's milk.

23 *on* = using.

26 *or one another:* i.e. to mate with one another!
blow me down: emphatic phrase expressing surprise.
they: i.e. the children.

28 *oh lord:* commonly used mildly emphatic expression of concern, doubt, despair, etc., prosodically supported here by the slow speed of utterance.

29 B's cat has just entered the room, to everyone's delight (bearing in mind the subject-matter of the narrative).

31–2 *they . . . litter:* note the colloquial order.

33 *crossed* = interbred, i.e. a mouse as one parent and a kangaroo as the other. Note the rising glissando (cf. 14 above).

38 *matter of fact:* i.e. unemotional, calm, and in this context, 'able to do something with mice' (cf. 36).

39 *Bridget:* A's other child.

40 *loo:* room containing the toilet—probably the most widely used of all the euphemisms for *toilet* amongst the south-east England middle-class.

41 *sweeping:* incomplete construction—probably intended as 'sweeping brush'.

42 *hoover:* normal term for 'vacuum cleaner' (from the name of the firm).

46 *what:* used here as a mark of hesitation indicating uncertainty about a following phrase of measurement.

51 *just:* the subject may have been elided, or A may be taking up the construction begun in 48.

56 *masses:* colloquial exaggeration for 'lots'.

58 Note the high pitch range and breathy articulation expressive of surprise and excitement. The height is maintained in the following lines, and the speed also increases. A further 'breathless' effect appears in 63.

61 *this:* A moves her hands rapidly in a zig-zag way.

go you know: go is often used, as here, to introduce the acting out of a specific *movement*, or the mimicking of a sound. The *you know* refers to the gestures A is making.

63 *off:* Note the dramatic effect obtained by holding the final consonant.

sleeky: sleek usually means 'smooth', 'glossy', but is also said of people, in the sense 'sly', 'insinuating'. It is not clear whether A intends any of the latter senses, but she is certainly using the word pejoratively here, as the slower speed and falling glissando pitches help to indicate.

65 *devised* = thought up, planned.

65–7 A is having some difficulty in identifying the cardboard core of the toilet roll, around which the paper is wrapped.

70 *slap* = place, put (colloquial), with the implication of suddenness and sharpness of contact, already noted in 5.18.

72 *however:* A puts on a comic voice quality, presumably in anticipation of some humorous point. But the effect is lost after the interruption.

73 Note the colloquial order.

81 *like mad:* colloquial intensifying phrase added to a verb, here meaning 'very energetically'.

94 *however:* used to indicate a return to the main theme. Cf. also 101.

98 Note the effect of the level tone as the second element of a compound tone: a 'warning' note is introduced into the dialogue. A presumably wants to get on with the story, and not be sidetracked into a point of detail: the tone is one of mild irritation.

107 *turned:* i.e. become fairly ripe, as shown by the colour.

EXTRACT 9

Farm holiday

This extract is taken from earlier on in the same conversation as Extract 4. A is at the beginning of her report about their summer holidays.

A but it was |very NĪCE| and |very RELĀXING|

B   so what |how did you 'map 'out your

DÀY| you |had your 'breakfast in the KÍTCHEN|

A   we |had our BRÉAKFAST|
(*laughs*) in the |KÍTCHEN| – and |then we 'sort of · ↑did 'what
. we LÍKED| and er |got 'ready to 'go ÓUT| (|M̄|) we |ÙSUALLY
'went 'out 'quite 'soon 'after 'that| – erm · the |children
were ↑álways ÙP| at the |crack of ↑DĂWN| · (|M̄|) with the
|FĂRMER| – and they |went in the MĪLKING 'sheds| and |helped
him 'feed the PĪGS| and |all THĪS| you |know we ↑didn't SÈE the   1
'children| – – and er |then we 'used to 'go ŌUT| |we – we had
|super ↑WÈATHER| – – |absolutely ↑SÙPER| – and |so we 'went to
a BĒACH| · |usually · for er but by a|bout ↑four o'clock it ·
we were ↑hot and we 'had to come 'off the BÈACH (|M̄| |M̄|) –
so we'd · |generally 'go for a TÈA 'somewhere| |just in 'case   1
↑supper was DELÁYED 'you 'know| (*laughs*) *laughs* and |then we'd
'get BÁCK| and the |children would 'go ↑straight 'back 'on to
the FÁRM| · (|M̄|) · and |have ↑PÒNIES| · their |ÒWN 'children
had 'ponies| and they'd · come |up and ↑put them on the
'ponies' BÁCKS| and er – and the |milking it was |MÌLKING   2
'time| and |RĔALLY| we were com|mitted to 'getting ↑BÀCK for
'milking 'time| (|M̀|) for the |CHÌLDREN| (|YÈAH| *laughs*) · and
'feeding ŪP 'time| and |putting the GĒESE to 'bed| and |all
THĪS| and erm · |one of the 'cats 'had KÍTTENS| and er |"oh
you KNÓW| |all THĪS 'sort of thing| · it |had them in a ↑big   2
'box in the ↑KÌTCHEN| in this |box of STRÀW| – |and erm – – ↑it
was just ↑GRÊAT| and |then we 'went BÁCK| you |KNÓW| and |they
had SÚPPER| and er |then we used to · 'get them 'into BĒD| and
· we w we g · she |got in an ↑awful ↑MÙDDLE| with |so 'many
↑PÈOPLE 'staying | with |some of the 'kids 'sleeping in a   3
CÀRAVAN| you |KNÓW| (*laughs*) |not ŌURS| but |HĒRS| · now sh a
she she's a |"VÈRY u'nïque 'type| |very 'very er 'upper
'middle 'class ÈNGLISH| (|YÈS| |YÈS|) you |SÉE| (|YÈAH|) – er
sort of the · the |general's DÀUGHTER 'sort of 'type| (|YÈS|
|YÈAH|) and |he was erm · from ↑ÈSSEX 'somewhere| (|YÈAH|) and   3
|he SWÒRE| *laughs* you'd |wake 'up in the ↑MÔRNING| and the

|ech |ringing 'down your ↑ears as he was 'swearing at the cōws|
or the |KĪDS| (|YÉAH|) or |SŌMETHING| (|YÉAH| |YÉAH|) – but
|very 'good 'natured wìTH it| erm (|YÈAH|) · but of |còURSE|
|when we 'came BÀCK| – |see sùSIE| |standing in the ↑GÀRDEN| 40
we had |very e'lite NÈIGHBOURS| |when we were 'in this 'little
HÒUSE| – you |bloody 'fool s STĒVEN| (*laughs*) *laughs* and |then
she *laughs* she |looks ùP| (|ÒH|) – |some 'bugger's ↑pinched
↑my ↑SPÀDE| (*laughs*) |and she ↑carried 'on 'like THÍS| the
|whole TÌME| (|YÈAH|) she was |back in SCHŌOL| (|YÈAH|) |and   45
we 'realized she just ↑didn't 'know 'what she was ↑sÀYING| you
|KNÓW| (|NÒ| |NÒ|) |cos I mean he ↑just SWŌRE 'like 'this| the
|whole TĪME| (|YÉAH|) w we *laughs* – |ÀNYWAY| she |soon 'got
ÓUT of it| · |Steven KNÈW he was SWÈARING| erm · but |Susie
↑just ↑DÌDN'T| you |SÉE| · and |SÒ| · |ÀNYWAY| – – they had a   50
|great TÌME| and er |we ↑really ENJÒYED it| you |KNÓW|

NOTES

1 *it:* i.e. the holiday.
2 *map out* = plan, arrange the events of.
3 *day:* i.e. what to do during the daytime.
  you had . . . : B is referring back to a point made earlier in the conversation by A.
8 *at the crack of dawn:* a fixed phrase meaning 'at daybreak'—a more
  vivid and dramatic alternative.
10 *see:* i.e. the parents were not being bothered by their children.
15 *a tea:* a rather unusual countable usage: A is referring to a particular
  kind of tea, where there was a fixed menu. One ordered, for example,
  'Three Devon teas, please', and this would be taken to mean a meal
  of scones, Devonshire cream, and jam, as well as the drink (of tea).
16 *laughs:* as discussed earlier in the conversation, supper was often late!
18 *their own:* i.e. the farm children.
19 *they . . . them:* the farmer's children would put A's children on the
  ponies.
23 *feeding up* = feeding. The *up* acts simply as an intensifier.
24–5 The slurred articulation reinforces the way A is listing events randomly, not intending to be precise.
24–6 The point about the kittens is really a digression. The narrative
  proper resumes in 27 with *and then.*
27 *back:* i.e. to the farmhouse.

29 *she* = the farmer's wife.
muddle = confusion; generally colloquial.
30 *kids* = children (colloquial).
31 *ours . . . hers:* i.e. the children.
32 *unique type* = distinctive type of person.
32–4 A is trying to characterize the rather eccentric, sophisticated, genteel personality of the farmer's wife (who incidentally spoke with a very 'far back' kind of Received Pronunciation). Note the slight change in A's own accent, and the generally slower tempo of her speech at this point.
35 *he* = the farmer.
Essex: a predominantly rural county to the north-east of London.
36 *swore:* note the drawled *s*, increasing the emphasis and thus suggesting that there is something special about the word.
37 *ech:* incomplete word (presumably 'echoes').
39 *with it:* colloquial construction used after predicative adjectives, meaning 'at the same time', 'as well'; i.e. the farmer is basically very good-natured, despite his swearing.
40 *see:* colloquial elision of the subject and auxiliary—presumably 'you would see'.
Susie: one of A's children.
41 *elite* = select, exclusive, fastidious.
we were in: i.e. A no longer lives there.
42 *you . . . Steven:* the lento prosody demarcates the utterance as a quotation—this is what Susie said to her brother (Steven). *bloody* is the most commonly used colloquial intensifier, but should be avoided by foreign learners of English unless: (a) they are on familiar terms with the others in the conversation, or (b) they wish to be strongly and seriously emphatic or offensive.
43 *looks:* note the switch to the present tense, as part of dramatic narrative.
bugger: strong term of abuse for a person (or, less often, an object). It would be considered offensive in any context other than one where the participants were on very intimate terms and the situation was informal.
pinched = stolen (colloquial).
47 *cos* = because (colloquial).
48 *got out of it* = lost the habit, stopped doing it.
50 *so:* summarizing use, indicating that A is coming to the end of her discourse. Note also the general slowing of tempo from 48 onwards.

EXTRACT 10

Sex education in schools

This is a further extract from the conversation introduced in Extract 3. It occurs early on in the conversation, at a

*point where the two men are still exchanging information
about their careers since leaving University. Not surpris-
ingly, in view of their professional interests, educational
problems have come to be discussed, and arising out of a
general discussion of the difficulties involved in teaching
teenage children, the conversation has come round to the
specific topic of sex education, as one way of attacking
some of the problems which these children present.*

*This topic had received a great deal of publicity in and
around 1970. The discussion ranged over such topics as
how and when matters to do with sex should be introduced to children, whose is the primary responsibility for
sex education (the parents' or the teachers'?), and, if the
subject is to be taught in school, how and in what degree of
detail is the information to be presented. This last problem
was especially acute, and the film referred to in line 7 was
one which had been made for use in schools, and which had
aroused a quite heated controversy because of the explicit
detail with which it described sexual behaviour.*

B but er · |you're 'teaching – erm at a GRÀMMAR school| |ÀREN'T
   you|

A |YÈS| · |YÈS|

B   well |what do you 'think about ↑SÈX edu'cation| – do
   you |think that er i it er I |mean · there's |been a a a   5
   'great ↑"HÒOha about it| (|M̌|) |RÈCENTLY| |HÀSN'T there| and
   erm – er about a |FÌLM that was 'made| and |só on| (M|HM̌|) – –
   well what |what are YÒUR 'views on it| – –

A |I find that – – 'with so ↑MÀNY of these 'problems| · |MÀRRIAGE|
   |SÈX edu'cation| · as |soon as you 'try and 'make it · a sort   10
   of ↑formal ↑LÈSSON| – – the |whole 'thing 'falls FLÀT| – –

B |M̌|

A you |KNÓW| |if you used to have a – – ↑period · |we used to
   'have one 'called DISCÙSSION 'groups| – – and you were |LÀNDED
   with| – – m |TWÈLVE| |SÌXTEEN| · |BÒYS| – |"in a RÒOM| · and   15
   |there you WÈRE| you were sup|posed to DISCÙSS| – |could be
   ÀNYTHING| – – but · |it was so ↑DÌFFICULT| it was |so
   ARTI↑FÌCIAL| ·

B |M̌|

A whereas · |teaching 'something like ↑èNGLISH of 'course| – a   2
|LÒT of 'these SÚBJECTS| |come up ↑fairly ↑NÀTURALLY| – |and
you can DIS↑CÙSS them| · |in the ↑CÔNTEXT of the 'class| ·
|"WHÈN they ARÍSE| – and |"ŬSUALLY 'then it be'comes| – |much
'more 'SATIS↑FÀCTORY| – – |and you get ↑LÒTS of 'questions|

B   I I · I |quite A↑GRÈE with 'that| 2
(|YÈS|) I mean it's a it's a it's a |WÌDE| sort of · |open
↑ÈNDED| |SÙBJECT ÉNGLISH| (|YÈS|) |ÌSN'T it| (|YÈS|) but the
|trouble is it ↑does de'pend on the ↑TÈACHER| because there
|are 'some 'teachers (|oh EN↑TÌRELY|) who ↑just – ↑WÒN'T| I
|mean as ↑far (|M̀|) as THÈY'RE CONCÉRNED| they they're |doing   3
a TÈXT| you |KNÓW| I |mean they're · they may be |reading
'something by ↑SHĂKESPEARE| (|M̀|) and |that's ↑ÌT| I er there's
|no ↑QUÈSTION |of EX"TÈNDING it in 'any 'way| (|NÒ|) and
|"ĂLSO| they |have their ↑own in ↑INHI↑BÌTIONS about 'talking
about 'sex| (of |CÒURSE|) I |mean they're ↑just not ↑FRÀNK   3
a'bout it|

A |YÈS| – |YÈS| –

B I |must say ↑I TĔND to be| I |mean I · you know I |do 'talk
↑quite ÒPENLY to my PÚPILS| which is – a |little ↑"DĂRING of
me| because the situ|ation in 'Cyprus is DÌFFERENT from HÉRE| 4
(|M̀|) I mean |people ↑ÀRE| a |bit ↑"NÀRROW in 'that re'spect|
you |KNÓW| they |don't LÌKE 'people to 'talk about it| |too
ÒPENLY| – but I |DÒ| because I |think it's IM↑PÒRTANT| but · the
|TRÒUBLE is| that erm · |that's ↑not 'really ↑SYSTE↑"MÀTIC| in
the |sense that ↑"Ì 'do it| but |how many ↑people – (|YÈS|)   4
|how many ↑"ÒTHER 'people 'do it| you |SÉE| ·

A |YÈS| i it's er it's an E|NÒRMOUS 'problem ÁCTUALLY| because
· as |soon as you ↑start to ↑make – er a ↑SPÈCIAL 'thing
a'bout it| – then IM|MÈDIATELY| – I |think you're cre↑ating
the ↑wrong ↑ÀTMOSPHERE| es|pecially for SÈX| ·   5

B |M̀| –

A be|cause – as ↑SÒON as it be'comes| |SPÈCIAL| – – |then it's

↑giving them in a 'sense the ↑WRÒNG 'attitude| –

B |YÈS|

A you |KNÓW| |this is 'some'thing   55

B   yes they're |"CÒNCENTRATING 'on it|

A |YÈS|

B |YÈS| ·

A |this is 'something that we've ↑got to 'look at ↑in a

   par'ticular ↑WÀY| (|M̆|) |ŌR| you |KNÓW| it's |CONTROVÈRSIAL| ·   60

   (|M̆|) where|as – ↑if it could be ↑TÀKEN| · |as sort of – –

   ↑part ÒF| – – |ÒRDINARY dis'cussion| or |part of ↑LÌFE if you

   LÍKE| |makes it 'sound a bit PÓMPOUS| (*laughs*) |but er – you

   |KNÓW| · |if it can be 'taken as – just ↑part of the ↑general

   – – ↑day to 'day ↑NÒRM| – – |then it's 'going to be ↑much   65

   ↑HÈALTHIER| – but as |soon as you 'start to 'make a 'SPECIÁLITY

   'of it| · |either by IG↑NÒRING it| · |or by par↑ticularly

   DISCÙSSING it| – – I think you're |going to cre'ate an

   UN↑NÀTURAL · 'attitude to'wards it|

B yeah I |think you ↑ÀRE| –   70

A it's |very ÀWKWARD| it's |"DÌFFICULT MÍND you| with a |class

   of THIRTY 'odd| – oc|casionally with the ↑SÈCOND 'form| – you

   |get – you |KNÓW| · well · we'll · we'll – |have erm – a DEBÀTE|

   – – (|M̆|) |what do you 'want to TÀLK a'bout| and |this is

   'something I |usually 'spend ↑one 'lesson · ar'ranging ↑what   75

   they 'want to TÀLK a'bout| and |then – ↑tell them to 'go away

   and ↑THÍNK a'bout it| and we – |have the dis'cussion a ↑later

   · a ↑later ↑LÈSSON| – and |often ENÒUGH| · |round a'bout the

   ↑SÈCOND 'form ||ÒH| · |"sex before MÀRRIAGE 'sir| or |just

   ↑"SÈX| or |SÈX in'struction| (|M̆|) or |should 'sex be 'taught   80

   in SCHÒOLS| you |KNÓW| – and – I |say all RÍGHT| · we'll |TÁLK

   about it| – and – – they |don't 'know · ↑what they're going to

   ↑SÀY| and they don't |RÈALLY 'know what · erm – – |what they're

   going to ↑talk about at ↑ÀLL| – but · you've |got · a ↑whole

   'lot of 'different ÀTTITUDES 'there| – |you ↑KNÒW| – as |soon   85

as it 'comes ÙP| that there's about – |half a DÒZEN 'little
BÓYS| · |who are PER↑HĀPS| – – a |little YÒUNGER than the
ÓTHERS| · or who |come from 'different ↑BÀCK'GROUNDS| – who
|"don't ↑"WÀNT to 'talk a'bout it| – and who are |rather · SHỸ|
and a |bit ↑FRÌGHTENED 'of it| – where|as you've got ↑ÒTHER   ⊊
'little BÓYS| (*laughs*) |who 'are – de↑cidedly AD↑VĚNTUROUS| ·
and |probably know every ↑bit as much a↑bout it as ↑ì do|
(*both laugh*) and er – |you've 'got this E↑NŎRMOUS| DIS|PÀRITY|
– and – it's |difficult to 'strike a BÀLANCE| – be|cause 'in
a ↑SÈNSE| if |you TĀLK| · if you |LÌKE| as |FRÀNKLY| |as the   ⊊
– ↑more ↑ÒPEN| |little BÓYS| A|BÓUT it| – |then 'you're ·
↑CLŎSING| the |ÒTHERS up| · |even ↑MÒRE| the |SHỸER ones| (|Ṁ|)
– are are |getting ↑more and 'more ↑"NÈRVOUS a'bout it in
'fact| and |you're cre'ating ↑"BÀRRIERS 'for them| – (but) whereas
|if ↑you 'talk a'bout it – – 'on ↑"THÈIR 'level| |or ↑try and   10
↑help ↑THÈM| – – |then the ↑ÒTHERS| are · are re|acting
A↑GÀINST it| it's er i it's |most PECÙLIAR|

NOTES

1 Note the high pitch range as B introduces a fresh topic.
6 *hoo-ha:* = uproar, controversy. The extra stress on this novel item
  is a common feature of both speakers in this extract. They are very
  much involved in their discussion, and are speaking persuasively;
  they therefore constantly give extra stress to words that they consider to be important for their argument, e.g. *usually* (23), *extending*
  (33), *daring* (39), *narrow* (41), *systematic* (44). In an argumentative
  or expository style, however, this process often comes to be extended
  to words of less specific importance, e.g. *in* (15), *when* (23). (In
  some varieties—such as television news reporting—this use of
  extra stress in trivial contexts has become so widespread that it has
  recently come to be much criticized.)
9 A introduces his response in a widely-used prosodic style: the high
  pitch, and generally slow articulation (note especially the drawled
  l and *f*) indicate that the speaker is giving careful and serious
  consideration to a topic. (It is commonly used on radio 'talk' pro-
  grammes, therefore to show that a speaker has thought deeply
  about a problem—even when he has not!)
10 *try and make:* quite normal in conversational English. There is

perhaps a tendency to use 'to' instead of 'and' in more formal speech. (See also 100.)

11 *formal lesson:* a lesson in which the same material is systematically worked through by the whole class as a unit led by the teacher. Lessons involving individual or group work on a number of different topics are often described as 'informal'.

falls flat: fails to make an impact, or engage attention, and therefore does not succeed in doing what it was intended to do.

Also in 11, note how the slow speed up to this point contrasts dramatically with the rhythmic emphasis of the final clause.

13 *period:* a designated unit in the school timetable, in which a particular subject or activity is followed. The word means the same as 'lesson'; but there is a tendency to use 'period' in secondary, and 'lesson' in primary education. (But see 78.)

14 *discussion groups:* a title is being quoted, which is also a new term in this conversation; hence the careful pronunciation.

you: note the informal use. Cf. 'one' in more formal speech.

landed with = presented with. This colloquial phrase always has an implication of external factors producing an unwilling response—'I had no choice'. Compare 'left with', and also other colloquial variants 'stuck with', 'saddled with', 'lumbered with'.

15–17 The low pitch range and creaky articulation have a diminishing force. A does not consider the actual number or topic important. The point he is making is the general one about artificiality (17–18): when he makes this point, therefore, the pitch rises sharply and his speed increases.

20 *of course:* as explained above, both speakers took an English degree; A is thus referring to their common knowledge.

22 *in the context of the class:* i.e. in relation to the literary theme or character which is the subject of the English lesson.

26–7 *wide, open-ended:* B is referring to the infinitely large number of subjects that could be raised under the heading of 'English'. *Open-ended* (antonym 'closed') = 'without any natural boundary'.

29 *won't:* i.e. will not allow such topics as sex to be introduced into the English lesson.

30–1 *doing a text* = analysing a set piece of literature.

32 *that's it* = that is all. They will merely read the text, instead of extending it.

33 *extending it* = relating it to everyday experience.

34 *in:* anticipating the first syllable of the following word.

inhibitions: inabilities to do certain things, as a result of psychological difficulties or fears.

35 *frank* = open, prepared to be truthful and explicit, forthcoming.

38 *tend to be:* i.e. frank about sex. *tend* = have an inclination, or tendency.

41 *narrow* = narrow-minded (antonym 'open-minded').

42 Note the low pitch range for the parenthetic remark. Again in 62–3.

44 *systematic:* an idiosyncratic use of this word, as B's explanation makes clear.

47 *enormous:* note the reduced loudness for emphasis; also in 48 (*special*).

48 *thing* = issue. The word is used in a number of current colloquialisms, e.g. 'I've got a thing about it' (= 'I have a strong liking for (or dislike of) something'; 'doing your thing' (= 'doing something which is characteristically suited to you, or which strongly appeals to you').

50 *especially for sex:* note the high pitch range and increased speed for the afterthought felt to be of particular interest.

59–60 *this is . . . controversial:* As the precise articulation helps to indicate, A is giving examples of statements representing 'the wrong attitude'; they are not *his* beliefs. Note especially the pronunciation of *a* (/eɪ/) in 59.

61 *sort of:* note the very rapid pronunciation here. (See p. 99.)

63 *makes:* normal omission of Subject. (See p. 104.)

64 *general* = usual, regular, routine.
   day to day = everyday.
   norm = average, normal situation.
   A is using a series of words of similar meaning as an expression of emphasis. The variable speed and rhythm with which he says the words suggests that no importance is being attached to the semantic nuances which differentiate them.

72 *thirty-odd* = about thirty. An informal usage, which in this case does not permit the antonym 'even'. (Note the alternative ways of indicating approximation in colloquial English, e.g. 'a class of, say, thirty' (or 'a class of thirty, say'), 'a class of round about thirty' (or '. . . thirty, round about'). For further examples see p. 113.) Note the potential ambiguity, if *odd* is over-stressed, in such sentences as *30 odd people were there* (= 'about 30 people' or '30 peculiar people').
   second form: the second year class in a grammar or secondary school, for the age-range 12–13.

73 *debate:* a formal discussion, following certain rules of procedure, a modified version of which is sometimes used in the classroom.

74–5 The common conversational practice of blending two similar constructions is seen here. What A says could be seen as involving a mixture of 'this is something I usually (do)' and '(I usually) spend one lesson . . .', illustrating a change in syntactic direction.

78 *a later lesson:* i.e. during a later lesson.
   often enough = quite often.

79 *oh . . .:* A adopts a resonant voice quality and a regional pronunciation (reminiscent of London) to draw attention to the fact that he is quoting from the children. However, he does not keep it up consistently for the whole of the quoted utterance.
   sir: the usual form of address to a male teacher. Compare *miss* for lady teachers. These items may also be used in clause structure, in informal speech, e.g. 'Miss is coming', 'Sir'll be along in a minute'.

Adult foreigners should note that *sir* is hardly ever used as a natural form of address in Great Britain (though it is widely used in the United States and in Ireland).

84–5 *a whole lot* . . .: the high pitch range and quieter articulation make this comment contrast with its context, and suggest that A sees the point as being particularly important.

86 *it:* i.e. the topic of sex.

comes up = is mentioned. (Compare similar phrases, such as 'is brought up', 'is broached', 'arises'.)

half a dozen: even without 'about', this phrase may imply vagueness —'more or less six'. (Compare *couple* in 2.30.) The phrase is always precise when buying objects, though, as in 'half a dozen eggs'.

88 *different backgrounds:* i.e. different kinds of home or social class.

92 *every bit . . . do:* 'every bit' is an optional emphatic phrase, meaning 'quite definitely'; cf. 'it's every bit as interesting as the other one'. It may also be used before the indefinite article, as in 'John's every bit an Englishman'.

93 *disparity* = difference; i.e. between the two types of child.

94 *strike:* one 'strikes' a balance. One may also 'keep' or 'maintain' a balance.

94–5 *in a sense* = in a way. The phrase does little more than express the tentativeness of the speaker.

95–102 A's difficulty in finding a solution is reflected here in his difficulty in summarizing the problem. His utterance breaks down initially, and again towards the end, into a series of short tone units, with frequent pauses.

97 *closing the others up:* used in the idiosyncratic sense of 'making it difficult for them to participate'. Note that 'open up' may be used in similar contexts, but with opposite meaning: 'I tried to get him to open up, but he wouldn't tell us anything'. Compare also 'shut up', and the colloquial variants 'belt up', 'wrap up', which are normally used only as imperatives or infinitives.

102 *peculiar:* here refers to the unusual difficulty presented by the situation; alternative items would be 'odd', 'funny', 'strange'.

EXTRACT 11

Christmas habits

This is a further extract from the conversational evening introduced in Extract 7. The participants have now begun to eat sandwiches (as may occasionally be heard). They are discussing Christmas, only two weeks away, and comparing their different ways of passing Christmas Day. B and C have read about the idea that the main meal of the day, Christmas Dinner, is more convenient to organize

if it is timed to take place in the early evening, instead of at
its traditional time of the middle of the day.

B did |YÒU 'read it in the 'Sunday TÍMES|

C |WHÀT|

B |on SÙNDAY| a|bout this ↑new – er the |idea of 'having ↑Christmas
- DÀY| that you · sort of get |up in the MÓRNING| and |have
your CÈREALS and 'whatnot| (C: |M̀|) – and |then about e↑leven
THÍRTY| (C: |CHRÌSTMAS 'cereals| A: |M̀|) – |ÒH| of |CÒURSE| · you
|have a BRÙNCH| – – – you |KNÓW|

A |nice SÀVOURY 'things| you |KNÓW| – |bits
of ↑nice · BÁCON| and · |all THÀT|

B SÂUSAGES| ∼∼∼

C   well you're |doing that
↑ÀNYWAY| |ÀREN'T you| you're sort of |supping 'all ↑MÒRNING|
laughs

B and you |have a · a ↑PRÒPER 'brunch|

A and |then you 'put your 'turkey ÍN|

B |"THÊN you 'put your 'stuff on| · and you |"ÈAT| – – li |in the
↑ÈVENING| (C: a|bout ↑sÌx or 'something| you |KNÓW|) |six ↑o'
CLÒCK or 'something| and you |eat ∼∼∼

C   in the |middle of BÍLLY ↑Smart's
↑CÌRCUS| ∼∼∼

B well |that's ÌT| er well of |CÒURSE| I |DÌD 'think of THÁT| ∼∼∼

A but |THÈN I 'mean| |isn't it a RE↑LÌEF| to |have an ex↑cuse
for ↑getting A↑WÀY from the TELEVÍSION| (B: YÈAH|) cos one
|tends to have

C and n n · |no ↑TÈA| – –
(A: ∼∼∼) |wait a MÍNUTE| I'm |just 'catching ↑ÙP on 'this
CONVERSÁTION| |no 'Christmas TÉA|

A   I can |see you have ↑PRÒBLEMS|

B |but yòu SĒE| · |nobody ever ↑ÈATS their 'Christmas tree| |TÈA|

C |TRÚE| –

|very TRÚE|

A   you |could have 'Christmas 'cake for ↑BRÙNCH| |CÒULDN'T you|

C – – |ÒH| I |don't know about THĂT|

B |YÈS| 35

C |mince PǏES| |CÈRTAINLY| ⁓

A |cos I ↑MÈAN| if they're |ĂDDICTS| · then they'll |eat it WHEN↑ÈVER it is|

B   be|cause you SĒE| they |eat their BRÉAKFAST| and then they're |stuffing all MÓRNING| and you · you |"slave   40
AWÁY| at (A: |YÉAH|) · you're |"RÙSHING| to |get this ↑Christmas DÌNNER| (A: well |that's what ↑I said to DÀVID|) for a · a ⁓ A|RǑUND| |LÙNCHTIME| you |KNÓW| with|in the ⁓ LÌMITS|

A   he |said ↑I 'never NÔTICE any
'rush he ↑SÁYS| *laughs*   45

B   well |you're not ↑DÒING it| |NÒ| – with|in the
'limits of LÙNCHTIME| and and

C   he's |always ↑BÒOZED by LÚNCHTIME| (*all laugh*)

B and and |then ↑nobody FÈELS like it| and |then you're FLÀKED| 50
for the |RÈST of the 'day| and then |everybody de'cides they're a bit ↑HǓNGRY| (A: |YÈAH|) a|round sìx| · and and you've |got to get ÙP| and you're you |KNÓW|

NOTES

1 *you:* B has previously been addressing A, and now turns to C, hence the nuclear tone on the pronoun.
Sunday Times: the name of a newspaper.
2 *what:* C has his mouth full, hence the muffled pronunciation.
4 *-Day:* B's eating rhythm introduces a pause, very abnormally, into this compound.
5 *cereals:* grain-based food, such as corn flakes, porridge or shredded wheat, usually eaten with milk at breakfast time.
and whatnot = and other things not necessary to mention (colloquial). There are many colloquial non-specific phrases of this kind, e.g. 'and things', 'and the like'.

6 *Christmas cereals:* C is suggesting that, being Christmas, there would be special types of cereal to be had that day!
oh of course: B responds to C's joke with good-humoured sarcasm, but does not let this interrupt her flow.

7 *brunch:* a blend of 'breakfast' and 'lunch' (colloquial)—usually referring to some kind of light meal taken mid-morning. The subsequent silence suggests that C is unclear as to what kind of thing is meant, and so B proceeds to amplify the notion, reinforced by A (who also has her mouth full, hence the slurred pronunciation).

8 *savoury* = appetisingly flavoured, especially with salt or spices.

11 *doing that:* i.e. eating (and drinking, it would seem from line 12).

12 *supping* = drinking (a colloquialism stemming from C's Northern background, and not generally used in the South).

14 *proper:* i.e. a planned snack (as opposed to the casual eating referred to by C).

15 *turkey:* the main item at a traditional Christmas dinner.
in: i.e. in the oven.

19–20 *Billy Smart's Circus:* for some years, a circus has been shown on television during the early evening, and this is one of the most famous ones. C is implying that his day is geared solely to watching the television; his tone expresses mock horror at the thought of anyone disturbing this routine.

23 *cos* = because (colloquial).

27 C's melodramatic articulation here—very resonant, slow and precise —suggests another mock reaction on his part. Christmas tea also has its traditional components (involving Christmas cake and mince pies—cf. 32), and *he* is not departing from a tradition so much enjoyed!

28 *you:* A is now addressing B.

29 *nobody ever eats:* i.e. because they are too full, having eaten a heavy Christmas dinner.

34 C's low pitch range reinforces his 'disparaging' tone.

35 *yes:* note the held *y*. B is responding with satisfaction to A's remark in 32.

37 *addicts:* the allusion is to drug-taking. The implication is that if people are so fond of Christmas cake that they are unable to do without it, then they should not object if they are given this in the morning.

40 *stuffing* = eating greedily.
slave = work intensively.

46 *you:* B says this to D (David), the 'he' of 45.
doing it: i.e. making the dinner.

48 *boozed* = drunk (colloquial). C is suggesting that this is why D never notices the rush referred to by A in 44–5.

50 *it:* i.e. the dinner.
flaked = exhausted, tired out (colloquial).

52–3 *got to:* note the colloquial pronunciation /'gɔrə/.

EXTRACT 12

Losing a tooth

*This extract occurs a little later in the same conversation
as Extract 11. B had begun to tell a story about how far
her children believed in Father Christmas, and fairies in
general, but had been interrupted. She now begins again,
signalling the fresh start with a loudly expressed 'anyway'.
(C's utterance in the background is irrelevant to the story,
and has not been transcribed.) It is a traditional story told
to children that when a tooth comes out, if it is left under
the pillow on their bed, fairies will come and exchange it
for money (usually a sixpence, in the old monetary system). The parents then take away the tooth during the
night, leaving the coin in its place.*

B |ÀNYWAY| – |Susie SĀID| – that · there were |no such 'things
  as FÁIRIES| |ÉLVES| |this 'that and the ↑ÒTHER| – |WÈLL| · the
  |night she ↑PÙT her 'tooth 'under the PÍLLOW| we for|got to
  'put the ↑MÒNEY there| and |take it A↑WÀY| we for|got all
  A↑BÒUT it| (A *laughs*) so she got |ÙP in the MÓRNING| – my   5
  |TÔOTH's all 'gone| and there's |no MŎNEY| – |Dave said well
  'there you ↑ÀRE you SÉE| |YÔU 'said| you didn't BE|LÌEVE in
  FÁIRIES| so |how can you ex'pect the ↑fairies to ↑come and
  ↑SÈE you if| – – |ÔH| but I |"DÔ believe in FÁIRIES| (D *laughs*)
  you |KNÓW| I |really DÓ| (A *laughs*) so |Dave said well · ↑try   10
  a'gain TONÌGHT| – – so |that NÍGHT| |thank 'goodness we
  RE↑MÈMBERED| (A *laughs*, C: |M̂| ⁓) so the |next MÓRNING| she |gets
  ÚP| |all HÁPPY| |"oh they've ↑BĒEN| they've |BĒEN| I've |got
  my MŌNEY| and |Dave said well ↑there you ÁRE| – – that |just
  SHÒWS| that you i if you |they hear you 'saying you 'don't   15
  BELÍEVE| · |no ↑MÒNEY| she |SĀYS| – she says |well · I ↑know
  you're 'only ↑SÀYING 'that| be|cause you for↑got to ↑PÙT it
  THÉRE| (*all laugh*) and |"NŎW| – |she ↑RÈCKONS| that · er ·
  she |SÁYS| · she |comes ÍN| and she'll |grin ↑all ŌVER| she'll
  say – |CÒURSE| – – t |just 'out of the BLŪE she 'said| I |do   20

BE↑LÌEVE in| |Father ↑CHRÌSTMAS you KNÓW| (A *laughs*) and
she'll |GRÌN| ～ from |ear to ÈAR| and it's |perfectly
'obvious that she ↑DÒESN'T| (C: |YÈAH|) · but she's |not 'going
to ↑SÀY it| |just 'in ↑CÀSE| (*all laugh*, C: |YÈAH|) |just 'in
↑CÀSE| the there's |no 'toys on ↑Christmas MÒRNING|

A |what ì 'like DÓING|
is is erm – |with the 'PAKISTÂNI 'children| and the |ÎNDIAN
'children| the |ÌNFANTS| when |their 'tooth falls ↑out in
'school and they ↑CRỲ| – and |if they've 'got enough ÉNGLISH|
I EX|PLÁIN to them| that |in ÉNGLAND| · *coughs* you |put it
↑under the PĬLLOW| (B: oh |YĒS| |YĒAH|) · and a |fairy will
↑CÒME| (C: |M̀|) · and will |give you · well |～ 'two and a
'half P̌| but |that 'sounds a bit ↑CRÙDE for a FÁIRY| (B: |YĒAH|
it DŌES|) |DÓESN'T it|

B oh |NŌ| |ÒUR FÁIRIES| |have to 'pay FÌVE|

A |YÈAH| |five PÈNCE| – and it's |so FÙNNY you 'see| and |I SÁY|
now you |must ex'plain ↑PRÒPERLY| to your |mummy and ↑DÀDDY|
– |what this ↑CÙSTOM is| |in ÉNGLAND| you |SÉE| and |then they
– they |go ÓFF| |clutching ↑this TÓOTH| – and they |come BÁCK|
the |next DĀY| – and they |SÁY| |oh ↑MÍSS| · |fairies 'come MÉ|
|fairies 'come MÈ| (*all laugh*)

NOTES

1 *Susie:* B's child.
2 *this . . . other:* one of many colloquial phrases expressing an un-
   specified quantity (e.g. 'and so on', 'and the like'). Compare 11.5.
6 *all gone:* the child was unable to see the tooth (though, as it happens,
   it was still there).
   Dave: B's husband.
9 *if:* unfinished clause.
   oh . . .: the louder and slower pronunciation signals the quotation.
10–11 *try . . .:* the sudden diminuendo to a more gentle tone introduces
   a dramatic contrast.
15 *they:* mispronounced, presumably because of the rush of the discourse at this point.
16 *no money:* normal colloquial elision of Subject and Verb.

she says: note the very fast pronunciation, especially on the second instance.

18 *reckons* = thinks (especially in a calculating way).

19–20 *she'll say:* another very rapidly articulated phrase.

20 *course* = of course (a common elision in colloquial speech). Note the high pitch range at this point, indicating a quotation.

out of the blue = quite unexpectedly.

said: note how B's tense fluctuates, as she takes various temporal points of view while telling the story.

22 *from ear to ear:* the usual idiom to express the idea of a very broad grin.

24–5 *just in case:* note the high, slow pronunciation—a common way of emphasizing this particular phrase.

26–7 *what I like doing is:* this sentence is not completed after the following adverbials.

Pakistani children: A is a teacher of immigrant children.

28 *infants:* i.e. the infant class—the youngest in a primary school.

tooth: note A's regional pronunciation /tʊθ/.

30 A's voice quietens, as she adopts something of the 'mysterious' tone used when telling the children.

32–3 *two and a half p:* the modern equivalent of the sixpence traditionally given for a tooth.

33 *crude:* an idiosyncratic use, implying 'mean, ill-mannered'.

36 *it's so funny:* i.e. the classroom situation.

EXTRACT 13

Sex films

This is another extract from the conversation introduced in Extract 1. It is in fact taken from just before the beginning of that extract, the topic of football being anticipated by a general discussion of why attendance at sporting events is so poor.

B SPEC|TÀTOR 'sports| are |dying ↑ÒUT ɪ THÍNK| (C: |YÈAH|) |people are · 'getting ↑CHÒOSY| the – – there's |more to ↑DÒ of CÓURSE| (A: |M̀|) – |more ↑CHÒICE| · |things have 'got ⌇⌇⌇

A   but i i is |that ↑ÌT do you THÍNK| or |is it the the ↑MÒNEY| that's erm – |being   5 ↑CHÀRGED|

B |I think

it's · I |think it's the ↑money they're ↑CHÀRGING| is |ÒNE
THÍNG| but I |think ĂLSO| erm – |people are ↑choosy about
↑what they ↑go to ↑SÈE| (C: |YÈAH|) and er – –   1

A |YÈAH| I SUP|PÒSE SÓ|

B   I |MÈAN| |"CÌNEMA| have b for a |LÒNG time| has |been in
TRŌUBLE| – I mean that's why well |you 'got ↑all these ↑SÈX
'films| – it was a |kind of a ↑desperate at↑tempt to

C   sh it's a |sure 'sign of   1
FÀILURE| |ÌSN'T it|

B |YÈAH|

C |once they re'sort to THÁT| |RÈALLY| ∼

B   they're · they're |TRỲING to| get them ∼

A |WHÀT| 2
|once you re'sort to ↑SĚX| · you |MÉAN| (all laugh)

C well it's · |some 'people re↑sort to ↑BÈER| laughs |NÒ| but
you |KNÒW what I MÉAN| i it to |MÉ| it's |ÀLWAYS been a
con'fession of 'failure|

B & C |YÈAH| 2

C you |KNÓW| tha the i it's |CHÈAP| is'n it's a |cheap way of
– – I er

B   it's |trying to 'get the ↑CRÒWDS in|

C   it's a CON|FÈSSION| – –
er |YÈAH| – to |MÈ| it's a con|fession of a ↑lack of a ↑STÒRY| 3
|ÌSN'T it| a lack of er (B: |YÈAH|) – you |KNÓW| |any ↑DÈPTH
RÉALLY| I've |ÀLWAYS 'thought THÍS| with · with |THÉSE 'things|
(A: |M̌|) – I |mean I'm not · you |KNÓW| I'm not d I |don't
'mean in in a ↑PRÙDISH sort of WÁY| but I mean it's when it's
(B: well |what 'happens) |when you 'get · a ↑BÌLL| which is ·   3
|SÈX| (B: |YÈAH|) |week 'in ↑week ÒUT| a |double ↑BÌLL| of x ·
what · |double x̌ or what'ever they 'call them NÓWADAYS|
(B: |YÈAH|) or is |that BÈER| |ǐ don't know| · |double ↑x
laughs |isn't that EX↑PÒRTERS' 'beer| · (A laughs) but you
|KNÓW| you |get it erm · you |get they |get them in ↑SPÀSMS| 4

and then |Nòw and AGÁIN| you get the |Sound of ↑mŭsic| and
|everybody ↑FLòcks| – or |even to the ↑James ↑BòND 'films| ·
you |KNÓW| |good 'quality FÌLMS| · er and then · A|GÀIN| you
· you get erm |half empty ↑THÈATRES| and you |look at the · a
↑double 'billing of this ↑RÙBBISH| – (A: |m̄|) |seems to Mĕ| there's a   45
con|fession of – ↑on the way ↑òUT THÉRE| that's what (A: |m̂|) |I
always ↑THÌNK|

NOTES

2 *choosy* = fussy, fastidious, critically selective (usually with a pejorative implication).

5–6 *being charged:* i.e. for entrance to see a game.

8–9 *I think . . . thing:* note the colloquial blend of two sentences here, the
first ending at *charging,* the second beginning at *the money.*

13 *got:* normal colloquial elision for 'have got'.

22 *well it's:* unfinished construction.

23 Note the change in speed as C tries to make a serious point.

26 *is'n:* unfinished construction.
Note the rounded vowels, reflecting the marked expression of disgust
C was wearing on his face at the time.

34 *prudish* = excessively proper, over-sensitive, or over-modest, especially about sexual topics.

35 *bill* = the advertised listing of films at a cinema. A *double bill* (36) is a
listing where two major films of equal prestige are being presented in
the same show. Alternatively, a *double billing* (45).

36 *week in week out* = continuously (with a suggestion of routineness
and tediousness).
x: C is intending to say 'X films', i.e. films which have been given an
X Certificate by the British Board of Film Censors. The old system of
film classification, which C is recalling, recognized three grades: 'U',
which could be seen by anyone; 'A', which children could see only if
they were accompanied by an adult; and 'X', which children under 16
were not permitted to see. Recently, however, this system had been
altered, and C is still unsure about the new categories, one of which
is 'XX' (double X).

37 Note the low pitch range and increased speed, indicative of parenthesis.

38 *beer:* 'double X' is also the name of a brand of beer.
I don't know: note the rapid colloquial pronunciation /də'nəʊ/.

39 *exporters:* not a very usual way of expressing 'for export'.

40 *they:* unclear reference, possibly meaning 'the general public', possibly
'the cinemas'.

them: i.e. the sex films.

in spasms: i.e. at regular intervals; all the cinemas seem to be showing nothing but sex films.

41 *The Sound of Music:* the name of a film musical.

42 *flocks:* i.e. comes in crowds to see it. (One normally talks about sheep 'flocking'.)

45 *double billing:* see 35.

46 *on the way out* = deterioration, decay, failure.

EXTRACT 14

Country life

This is a further extract from the conversation used in Extract 6. The discussion of London found there arose out of a contrast between town and country life, the beginning of which is transcribed below. B's parents were just about to move house from London to a town in Kent (the 'it' referred to in line 1). (Detailed variations in B's speaking style—in particular her wide pitch range, varying tempo, and generally breathy quality—are not discussed in the commentary.)

B |I don't know 'what it ìs ABÓUT it| it · always |strikes 'me as
   – ↑slightly ↑MÈSSY| I |"LÌKE KÉNT| but I pre|fer ↑SÙSSEX| er
   I |don't know 'what the ↑subtle 'difference in the 'countryside
   ĭs| (|Ṁ|) |but ↑there's ↑SŎMETHING| – –

A |YÈS| |Sussex has – ↑super HÈATH 'country| (|Ṁ|) |lovely ·
   |lovely 'sort of 'rolling HÈATHS|

B   and the |"DÒWNS| (|YÈS|) you |KNÓW| · erm well
   th |there you 'see I 'mean the ↑WÈALD is LÓVELY| and and I m
   |LÒVE where| m |MÀRGARET GÓES| tha er |that 'I can ↑STÀND| but
   – |it's a · |I · I can |see it 'in my MÌND| |what it ìs| i it's
   the sort of |"VÌSUAL 'aspect| of the |CÒUNTRY| – erm |which I
   ↑half LÍKE| but there's |half 'something – – |perhaps it's not
   MÈLLOW e'nough| · and |yet wha |what could be 'more MÈLLOW|
   than |KÈNT| I |I ↑don't KNÒW| it's it's sort of |FŬNNY| · but
   er it |it's 'just a PÈRSONAL re'action 'to it| and ·

PAR|TÌCULARLY| · |I'm ↑thinking 'of this VÌLLAGE| |where my
↑aunt and ÙNCLE 'live| |which is ↑just 'out'side 'Tunbridge
WÉLLS| and |that – – erm |I 'wouldn't · well |I wouldn't live
'there for the WÒRLD| (*both laugh*) |although ↑STẴYING 'there|
|I EN↑JÒY it| be|cause at ↑least it ↑is 'in the CÒUNTRY| and   20
it's |rather ↑LÒVELY| – |but erm ·

A |Î couldn't 'live| in |ẪNY 'village| (|M̆|) for |ẪNYTHING| I ·
I was |brought ÙP in one| and – – |"DRÈADFUL| f sort of
|claustro'phobic ↑places they ↑ÀRE|

NOTES

1 A new direction to this conversation is signalled by the high pitch
level of the opening words.
strikes me = seems to me. This phrase often has pejorative implications; for example, one would be more likely to hear' It strikes me
she's been very careless' than 'It strikes me she's been very careful'.
2 *messy* = untidy, chaotic. B is using the word in a rather idiosyncratic way: it is unclear from the context what exact qualities she
means.
Kent: the county in the south-eastern corner of England.
Sussex: the county immediately to the west of Kent.
5 *super* = of excellent quality. This informal emphatic adjective is in
very common use nowadays, especially among young people of the
middle class or above, and favoured more by women than men.
heath: an adjectival use of the noun, which means a stretch of open
uncultivated land, usually covered in grass, heather, shrubs, etc.,
with perhaps a few scattered trees.
7 *the Downs:* ranges of grass-covered chalk hills in south-east England. The North Downs are not far from London, chiefly in Kent
and Surrey, and the South Downs are near to the south coast, in
Sussex. The noun 'downs' can be used to refer to any undulating
and treeless hilly areas, not solely to those found in the south-east.
In this general sense, the initial capital is not used.
8 *the Weald:* an area of country lying between the North and South
Downs.
9 *stand* = put up with, tolerate (a rather strange choice of word for
this context).
10 *in my mind:* i.e. in my imagination—compare 'in my mind's eye'.
11 *visual aspect:* a (rather formal) reference to the scenic qualities of
the area of Kent that is being discussed.
12 Note the meditative tone, signalled by the gradual slowing down
and softer level of the utterance; it contrasts sharply with the

increased speed and loudness of the following line, where B's attitude is more decisive.

13 *mellow:* not a very precise adjective in this context. The word always has pleasant connotations, especially 'free from roughness or harshness', 'mild and pleasing', 'fully matured'. The adjective is used especially with reference to (a) qualities of fruit (*mellow peaches*, i.e. fully matured, soft, sweet peaches); (b) gentleness achieved through experience or age (usually as a verb) (*he mellowed*, i.e. lost his harshness); (c) qualities of sounds (e.g. *the mellow tones of the clarinet*, i.e. free from harshness or stridency); (d) qualities of objects (*mellow look*, i.e. tasteful, soft in appearance, free from garish colours or decoration). It may also be used to refer to someone who is of a pleasant, convivial disposition or behaviour, especially when this is induced by liquor (*You're very mellow this evening*).

14 *funny* = strange, peculiar.

17 *Tunbridge Wells:* a town in Kent.

18 *and that:* unfinished construction.

18–19 *well . . . world:* the breathy, tense and piano articulation strongly reflect B's shocked attitude. A similar effect is used by A in 23–4.

19 *for the world* = on any account (i.e. (not) for (all the wealth in) the world). Compare other such phrases: 'for worlds', 'for anything' (see 22), (not) for all the tea in China, 'if you paid me'.

19–20 *staying there I enjoy it:* unusual word order for emphasis, i.e. 'I enjoy staying there'.

22 *for anything* = on any account (cf. 19).

23–4 *dreadful . . . are:* inverted word order for emphasis.

24 *claustrophobic places:* places which are likely to give one a feeling of claustrophobia, i.e. a fear of confined spaces.

EXTRACT 15

Family grouping

This extract is taken from earlier on in the conversation used in Extract 4, but at a point where A and B are the sole participants. They have been comparing ideas about the education of young children, and A has asked B (who is a primary school teacher) what she feels about the method of organizing children into classes known as 'family grouping' (other names for this method are also in use). Traditionally, a child changes his teacher and class in the primary school each year as he grows older; but in the family grouping method, a child stays for more than one year in the same class with the same teacher, working alongside other children who may be a year older or

*younger than he is. The relative advantages of the two
approaches have been hotly debated. In the present
extract, A is worried, because the school which her
daughter attends is proposing to change its system to the
family grouping method, and she is wondering how her
daughter will be affected.*

B well I re|member 'Dave 'rang me ↑ÙP a'bout this 'business|
  (|YÈS|) of |changing to 'family ↑GRÒUPING| – and erm – – – er
  you |KNÓW| it de|pends on ↑so 'many THĪNGS| |RĔALLY| · but |I
  have · |this 'friend of 'ours who 'lives er erm 'over the
  'other 'side of RÉADING| you |KNÓW| ·   5
A |oh YÈS| –
B |she · erm – – |she 'teaches 'somewhere 'over THÁT 'side| I
  |don't 'quite 'know WHÉRE| – – but |she's ↑TÈRRIBLY a'gainst it|
  (|ís she|) |she's a 'far · ↑more ex↑perienced ↑infant 'teacher
  than ↑ĭ 'am| you |KNÓW| (|YÈS|) I |mean I've 'only · been   10
  'doing ↑infant 'teaching for a ↑SHÒRT 'while| – but |she won't
  have ↑ÀNYTHING to 'do with it| be|cause ↑SHÈ 'says| that it ·
  |puts ↑too 'much 'strain on the ↑TÈACHER|
A I'm |SÛRE it 'does| –
B erm · it's it's |all RÌGHT| |in a 'small GRÓUP| (|M̄|) for   15
  |children it's a ↑great I↑DÈA| (|YÈS|) – but er |most of us
  ↑haven't 'got 'small GRÓUPS| (with |forty KÍDS| · |YÈS|) and
  it |puts a ↑terrible 'strain on the ↑TÈACHER| – |so that · you
  KNÓW| |you 'can't get ↑ÀNYBODY| (|M̄|) to the re|quired
  ↑STĂNDARD| be|cause you 'just – have 'got ↑so many ↑GRÒUPS| –   20
  do you |understand 'what I MÉAN| (|yes I ↑DÒ| |YÈS|) |if
  you've 'got a 'whole CLÀSS| at the |same ĂGE| · |you will
  HĀVE| (|YĒS|) · |by NĀTURE| you will |HĀVE in it| at |least (|M̄|)
  ↑three GRÓUPS |(|M̄|) |maybe MÒRE| – now |if you've 'got –
  "THRÈE 'different ÁGE 'groups| (|YÈS| |three ÁGE 'groups| ·   25
  |YÈS|) you've |got at 'least ↑NÌNE 'different GRÓUPS| (|YÉS|)
  |HÀVEN'T you|

A |YÉS|

B you |KNÓW| · |even ↑THÒUGH 'some of 'them 'might 'work 'up with
a| (|YÉAH|) · a |higher GRÓUP| yóu've |STÌLL 'got a LÓT|

A |M̄|

B |and it 'does 'put a tre'mendous STRÁIN| you |KNÓW| (|YÈS|)
it's |terribly ↑DÌFFICULT|

NOTES

1 *business* = matter, state of affairs.
3 *it:* i.e. whether it succeeds or not.
4–5 *the other side:* the conversation is taking place in Reading.
6 *yes:* note how the falling tone here suggests that A has already
heard of this person.
15–16 *for children . . . .:* note the inverted word order for emphasis.
17 *kids* = children (colloquial).

3

Linguistic Analysis

We propose now to look at conversational English, as exemplified by
the above extracts, and point out some of its most important linguistic characteristics. It seems useful to organize what we have to
say under three general headings: fluency, intelligibility, and appropriateness. These are the main factors which we feel need to be
considered in assessing the success or otherwise of conversational
speech.

A. *Fluency* is a highly complex notion, which we here relate
mainly to smoothness of continuity in discourse. It thus includes a
consideration of how sentences are connected, how sentence patterns
vary in word-order and omit elements of structure, and also certain
aspects of the prosody of discourse.

B. *Intelligibility* essentially depends on the recognizability of the
words and sentence-patterns of speech. It therefore involves us in
considering the phonetic character of conversational English,
particularly from the point of view of its segmental (vowel and
consonant) system.

C. *Appropriateness* refers to the suitability of language to situation. In this book, we use it primarily to talk about the way in which
informality is expressed by choice of vocabulary, idiom, and syntax.

It is not possible to make an exhaustive study under each of these
headings. What we have done is select one area of language use for
detailed analysis under each heading, and refer to certain other areas
in less detail. All of the illustrations are taken from or adapted from
the above extracts, or from other parts of the tapes of which they
form a part.

Before beginning our detailed analysis, it is important that we
clarify three central terms—*conversation*, *discourse*, and *utterance*.
It is sometimes forgotten that these are technical terms, and need
careful definitions if any approach is to be consistent and teachable.

We therefore propose the following senses for these terms. A *conversation* is any stretch of continuous speech between two or more people within audible range of each other who have the mutual intention to communicate, and bounded by the separation of all participants for an extended period. The weakness in this definition of course is that we cannot define our notion 'extended period'. A brief interruption (for instance, someone going to answer the phone and returning) we do not consider sufficient to produce two separate conversations; and it is perfectly possible for a group to split up and 'continue the conversation' in a different place later. But after a day or so's separation, one would hardly want to talk about the 'same' conversation. This issue does not affect any of the material we have chosen to analyse; but it is worth remembering that it exists. Within conversation we recognize the notion of *discourse*, which is a continuous stretch of speech preceded and followed by an agreed change of speaker. The word 'agreed' is needed so as to discount brief interruptions, agreement noises, and so on, which only temporarily 'interrupt the flow'; but again, a precise definition of what constitutes 'agreement' is hard to come by, and we have not tried to give one here. Within a discourse, lastly, we call any stretch of speech which we wish to isolate for analytic purposes a *focal utterance*, often simply *utterance*. An utterance may therefore be anything from a morpheme (or even a meaningless noise) to a string of sentences.

A Fluency

In the world of written English, discourse has a regular, predictable pattern of connectivity. Sentences are regularly identifiable, commencing with a capital letter, and concluding with a clear mark of punctuation—apart from in a few definable cases where these rules may be broken (such as in literature, or advertising). The general impression is one of premeditation and conscious organization. Errors of expression and changes of mind, if they occur, can be carefully erased, and eliminated from a final draft. If a word or phrase does not come to mind, the writer may pause until he finds it, or choose some alternative. The page you are reading now is errorless: it does not show the various stages of revision from manuscript to printer's proof which gave it the form it now has. Only informal letter-writing and one's own notes to oneself tend to preserve the evidence of the flexible organization which comes with spontaneous expression.

The main factor which distinguishes written from spoken language, in this respect, is time. In writing, there is always time to revise, to re-write; in speech, there may be a chance to pre-plan expression, by using notes, or memorization, or reading aloud. But in the immediacy of spontaneous speech, on informal occasions, the possibility of producing regular and tightly controlled discourse becomes remote. Nor, on informal occasions, is there any real need or desire for such controlled or careful speech. Controlled or careful speech, after all, must be a product of a controlled or careful speaker; and if one then asks why is such a speaker being so controlled and careful, the answer would normally be: 'Because the situation demands it'. But situations in which controlled and careful speech is the norm are precisely *not* those which we mean when we talk about informal conversational English. The 'informality' of conversation is identified primarily by the *absence* of external pressures to talk along predetermined or rigid lines, as we suggested in the Introduction. It is a use of language where—apart from certain restrictions on subject-matter—it does not matter what happens, because there is no one present who will criticize. Thus we find a casualness, a randomness about the subject-matter and construction of informal conversation; and this regularly leads to loosely co-ordinated constructions, incompleteness, ungrammaticality, stylistic vacillation, and many other linguistic 'errors'—but these features remain either unnoticed or tolerated, and can be called errors only from the viewpoint of the norms of formal or written language. The person who tries to be correct on these informal occasions is pedantic; the person who maintains a façade of linguistic formality rapidly becomes a bore.

In informal conversation, then, where there is no time or need to plan far ahead, what linguistic features should we expect to encounter? In what ways may fluency be maintained, without contravening our desire for informality? The short answer is that there are very many such ways, and that we do not know what all of them are, for no exhaustive analysis has ever been carried out. But it is not difficult to see what the most frequently used features of discourse-building are: all the categories in the following classification are well represented in the data above.

The simplest model of a conversational interaction requires two speakers, which we here name A and B. We will assume that when A and B come into contact, A decides to speak first. Theoretically, we see this utterance as containing three components: language which *initiates* the utterance; language which indicates that his utterance is *continuing*, not yet completed; and language which indicates that he *has finished* speaking. (There may of course be factors other than language which indicate these functions, such as gestures and facial expressions; but we will concentrate on the linguistic features.) B may then respond to A, in which case there may be specific *response* language, followed by the same three components as in A. A may then repeat B's cycle; and so on.

Connectives

We are not in this book going to study the range of linguistic features which may act as initiators in conversations; these, such as types of greeting, 'phatic' comments about the weather or health, and so on, we must leave for some other occasion of study, The present focus of attention is on the question of how the *continuity* of utterance is maintained, once it has been initiated. Let us assume, then, that an utterance-initiating structure has been used by A, who wishes to develop his point in some way. A number of possibilities suggest themselves.

The most obvious continuity feature is simple *addition* of another structure, itself grammatically independent, using a conjunction. In conversation, a very large proportion of simple addition is effected by the use of 'and', which adds nothing to the meaning of the linked structures, and distributes the emphasis evenly throughout the utterance, as in Extract 5, or the following example taken from Extract 2 (lines 7–13):

> it was a huge bonfire . . . and the bonfire was right under . . . and I was so worried the . . . and I was so worried . . .

This straightforward process of addition is learned very early in the language acquisition process. Children of three and four tell their first stories by stringing their clauses together with *and*; and teachers have great difficulty inculcating alternative forms of connectivity in the written expression of their pupils in secondary schools. Semantically speaking, it is the most neutral kind of connectivity that there is. From the foreigner's point of view, the important point to note about it is that to perform this neutral function the *and* is generally given an acceptable weak form. This may be achieved by reducing either the beginning of the word, or the end, or both, as follows: /nd/, /ən/, /n̩/. The first is only usual before a vowel. One should also remember that /n/ becomes /m/ before bilabial plosives and /ŋ/

before velar plosives. Avoiding the appropriate assimilation is likely to disturb the rhythmic fluency of the utterance. Note however that if one wishes to hesitate on the conjunction—a particularly common occurrence in informal conversation—it is the strong form of pronunciation which is used, with the vowel extended in length (e.g. 10.14, and many other places).[1]

In all these cases, the use of *and* is optional; leaving the word out will not produce a grammatical error, or a problem of intelligibility; but the utterance would thereby become considerably disjointed, and sound abrupt, with corresponding implications for the fluency of the conversation. One might try leaving out these conjunctions, and judging the effect that results. One should not, however, go away with the impression that the addition feature must always be in sequence with the other sentences. It usually is, as in the case of *and*, or the use of the dash in informal writing; but in speech the use of a rising or a narrowly falling intonation on the initiating sentence (often followed by a pause) may suffice to indicate continuity, (e.g. 1.12). Another example of a neutral addition feature, particularly common in narratives, is *then*, in its weak form /ðən/.

Simple addition is of course a quite familiar notion, and will already have been introduced to English students in the earlier stages of learning the language. Apart, then, from noting its frequency of occurrence in conversations, and recognizing it as a very useful way of connecting sentences in informal English, we do not feel that it is necessary to attempt to elaborate what is basically a simple syntactic feature. We shall therefore concentrate on the more complex notions involved in types of sentence sequence, where one does not simply add sentences together in this 'neutral' kind of way, but introduces some kind of semantic contrast between the sentences—some kind of orientation which will guide the listener as to the direction in which the conversation is intended to go, the intentions underlying what is said, or attitudes towards him. This is done by the use of a connecting word or phrase—usually an adverb or adverbial phrase or clause, but sometimes a short, parenthetic sentence. It is possible to distinguish three main functions of these connectives—though as we shall see, the boundaries between these functions are sometimes obscure.[2]

1. All cross-references to the extracts follow the convention: Extract Number. Line Number(s).
2. Quirk *et al.* (1972) have a more detailed analysis of adverbial connectivity which parallels ours to some extent (cf. their analysis of *conjuncts*, § 8.89, ff.).

(a) The connectives are interpreted as reinforcing, or specifically supplementing, the whole or part of the meaning of what has immediately preceded. One takes what has been said and builds upon it in various ways. The reinforcement may take the form of a complete repetition of what has just been said, or a paraphrase of it, or it may add a fresh piece of information arising out of it: these three possibilities may all be exemplified from the extracts, e.g. *in Sussex we did —in fact I went to one last week* (2.3). Other reinforcing connectives are: *as a matter of fact, to be precise, to be specific, in other words, as I say, that is, I must say, really, for instance, in a sense.* It is possible to group these into further semantic classes (as in Quirk *et al.*, 1972), but for the moment we propose to leave them as all falling within the general heading of 'reinforcement'. *And* may also reinforce in this way, it should be noted, whenever it is used as a separate tone-unit (usually with a rising or a falling-rising tone) or given extra prominence, e.g. *I got the jam*—AND *I didn't forget the bread. Or* is also used as a convenient means of introducing a paraphrase, as in *you'd better ask Jones to come—or 'big John' as he's usually called.*

(b) The connectives may be interpreted as *diminishing*, or retracting the whole or part of the meaning of what has preceded. A good example occurs in 2.1: *we're looking forward to bonfire night—at least the children are.* Other examples would be *or rather, at any rate, actually. Mind you* has this force in one of its uses (see below, p. 100), and *I mean*, likewise, can be used with a diminishing force.

Some general points about reinforcing and diminishing connectives should be noted. First, some of them are ambiguous, in that they are sometimes used with a positive, reinforcing sense, and sometimes with a negative, diminishing one. Examples are *I mean to say*, and *that is*, as follows:

> I'm going to borrow John's book—that is, if he'll let me.
> I'm going to borrow John's book—that is, I'm going right now.

The ambiguity is usually clearly resolved in speech, due to a clear prosodic contrast which distinguishes the two types of connective. The reinforcing phrases are generally pronounced in a higher pitch-range or more loudly than the preceding part of the sentence; the diminishing phrases, by contrast, are generally in a lower pitch-range or softer.

Secondly, all connectives are generally spoken with a falling-rising or rising intonation. To say them with a falling kind of tune would give an impression of seriousness or abruptness, which may of course be intentional, but which is usually more appropriate for formal discussion or domestic argument. There are however some more subtle prosodic contrasts to be noted in connection with the third category of connectives discussed below.

Thirdly, there are some particularly productive kinds of connective which may be illustrated from the extracts, most of which are reinforcing in meaning. One frequent construction is represented by *the trouble is*. This is commonly used to impose a level of organization on a conversation that has been meandering, or to give it a fresh direction. Phrases of this kind say, as it were: 'a lot has been said so far, but the main point we ought to concentrate on is the following . . .' The choice of noun indicates the speaker's attitude—whether he sees the issue as a problem, or whatever else he thinks about it. Other examples are: *the idea is, the question is, the answer is, the problem is, the solution is, the point is,* and the non-specific *the thing is.* This is very close to the common way of summarizing a discourse using initial adverbial phrases of the kind: *on the whole, in short, to sum up, (to put it) in a nutshell, in brief, all in all, to cut a long story short.* Note also the way in which some connective adverbials, e.g. *frankly, unfortunately, luckily, sadly,* merge with the more usual kinds of adverbial, which may have a verb-modifying function. There is rarely ambiguity between the sentence-connecting and verb-modifying functions of these adverbials in informal speech. One may hear contrasts such as

|SĂDLY| he |SÀID it| and |SÀDLY he said it|,

the first meaning 'it is unfortunate that he said it', the second meaning 'he said it in a sad way', but the second is uncommon in informal speech, and there is usually a fairly clear intonation contrast, which would only be lost in rapid utterance.

(c) The third category of connecting phrases is so different from the first two that they perhaps ought to be taken separately. The difference lies in the fact that, whereas so far we have been discussing only those connectives whose primary purpose is to make a clear semantic contrast between sentences in sequence, the following words and phrases have an additional, largely stylistic function, and sometimes little clear content. Their function is similar to the above, in that they are introduced into speech in order to maintain the continuity of discourse; but very often this is a secondary role. Their primary role seems to be to alter the stylistic force of a sentence, so as to express the attitude of the speaker to his listener, or to express his assessment of the conversational situation as informal. For this reason we refer to them as *softening* connectives, or *softeners*, for short. Quirk *et al.* refer to them as 'comment clauses' (§ 11.65). Examples are *you know, I mean, sort of, you see*, and the like. They express a wide range of nuances, and it seems impossible to make any satisfactory generalizations to cover all of them. For this reason, we propose to take them one at a time and discuss their main syntactic, phonological and semantic roles. However, we are aware that a great deal more research needs to be done before we can be absolutely certain about all the functions of these softeners. The following pages are primarily intended to account for the range of usage presented in the extracts, and should not be taken as an exhaustive classification.

(i) *you know*

This phrase may be used initially, medially, or finally in an utterance. Initially it appears only in statements, as in

you |KNÓW| I |think we ought to go òUT this 'evening|.

Medially it may occur in both statements and questions, but always at a point of major grammatical junction, as in

it was |CLÈAR you KNÓW| that he |wasn't going to DÒ it|.

In final position, the phrase usually occurs in statements, as in

he |won't 'want you to 'ring him ÙP you KNÓW|.

In all positions, the vowel of *you* tends to be reduced in quality: /jə'nəʊ/ or /j'nəʊ/. Sometimes it is articulated so quietly as to be inaudible. (In orthography, one may see *y'know*.) Also, the phrase is normally spoken as a separate tone-unit, with a rising tone on *know*. (In rapid speech in initial position there may be prominence alone, as in 2.29; but this is uncommon.) If these prosodic effects are not made, there may be confusion with other constructions. Compare, for example,

(i) you |KNÓW| he |works on sÙNdays|
(ii) you |know he 'works on sÙNdays|.

The second sentence means 'you are aware of the fact that he works on Sundays', whereas the first means something like 'oh by the way— he works on Sundays'. The distinction is not always clearly made in rapid speech, but the possibility for making this contrast is always there. The opposition is essentially between full vs. weak pronoun articulation, and separate vs. integrated intonation of the phrase.

The intonation and meaning of the phrase varies somewhat, depending on its position within the utterance. In initial position, firstly, it tends to be high and rapidly articulated, as in

you |KNÓW| |I've been 'thinking that . . .

where the phrase is likely to be either •✓ or •✓ , the whole phrase being in a higher pitch-range than the speaker's norm. It is optional whether a pause follows. If one does, it may be lengthy; and one should note that in such circumstances the speaker would not normally expect to be interrupted. The basic meaning of the phrase here is 'Wait a moment, I'm thinking, and you'll probably find what I have to say is interesting'. Without the pause, it is simply a polite, informal way of attracting attention or softening the force of what follows—a kind of vocal expression of sympathy for another's position. It is thus a phrase whose use is largely of stylistic importance.

In medial position in a sentence, the phrase tends to be spoken within the normal pitch-range, the tone-unit being of the same form as above, as in

I'm |going to the SHÒP NÓW| – you |KNÓW| the |one on the ↑CÒRNER|.

It is normal to have the *you* at a higher pitch level than that of *know*. In this use the phrase takes on a diminishing force. Its meaning is to indicate that the speaker feels some part of what he has already said to be unclear or ambiguous; the *you know* introduces a fresh attempt to get his meaning across, or to explain some aspect of his meaning further. It does not literally mean 'you are aware', though if spoken slowly it may take on this literal force. It is more like a hesitation noise which warns the listener that some re-planning is going on. This use may also be found initially in a sentence immediately after another speaker has interjected a query, as in

A I'm |going to get the TÌCKETS|
B the |TÍCKETS|
A you |KNÓW| the |CÌRCUS 'tickets|.

The medial use may also take on the pronunciation and function of uses (d) and (e) below.

In final position, there are many possibilities of pronunciation.

(a) The main medial pronunciation may be used, with the same effect.

(b) The tone may be 'run into' the previous unit, as in

he |didn't want THÀT you KNÓW|.

This has the meaning 'Are you not aware?' or 'Don't you remember?' The speaker is letting someone else know that he, the speaker, knows something the other does not. Depending on the circumstances, then, it is extremely easy to give offence when using this pattern, if the listener does not wish to be reminded, or if he thinks the speaker is being superior by so doing. Said with a smile, and a low rising tone, it is usually safe enough.

(c) With a high rising tone in a high pitch range, the phrase has a similar effect to one of the functions normally associated with tag questions, inviting the listener to agree with what has been said, or at least expressing the speaker's assumption that the implications of what he has been saying have been understood, as in

so then we |all 'went to the 'office by the 'main GÀTE| you |KNÓW|.

In this case, the pitch level of *you* is below the onset level of the nuclear tone.

(d) With a stress on *you* and a low rising tone, often drawled, this phrase in final position takes on some literal force, acting almost as a reduced form of a sentence such as 'Surely you must know'. It may even be used separately, or repeated *after* the sentence to which it was originally attached. For example,

I've |just been to 'see Mrs JÒNES| and – |you KNÓW|.

This indicates that it is unnecessary for the speaker to complete what was begun, because he assumes that the listener is quite aware of the point at issue. The implication, of course, is that there is something about Mrs Jones which is interesting or significant or scandalous, which need not be gone into, and which perhaps *ought* not to be gone into! This use presupposes common knowledge, a shared background of experience; (if the speaker has mistaken the extent of his listener's knowledge, he will be told so by, for instance, the response 'No, I don't know; what about her?'). This version of the phrase thus presupposes some degree of intimacy, and as a result is only likely to be used in informal situations. It is frequently accompanied by some appropriate kinesic feature, e.g. winking or nudging.

(e) With a relatively high unstressed *you*, followed by a wide drop in pitch to a low, often drawled falling tone, the implication is one of irritation—either at one's own inability to express something clearly or at the listener's inability to comprehend. In this sense, the phrase may even substitute for a lexical item, with the first tone-unit incomplete, as in

I'm |looking for the – you |KNÒW|.

(ii) *you see*

This phrase may be used initially, medially or finally in an utterance. Initially, as in

you |SÉE| there's a|nother SÌDE to all 'this|.

Medially, as in

I'm |VÈRY 'pleased| you |SÉE| that |John de'cided to CÓME|.

Finally, as in

they should |ask for PERMÌSSION you 'see|.

In all positions, the vowel of *you* tends to be reduced in quality, producing /jə'si:/ or /j'si:/. In rapid or abrupt speech, *you* may be omitted altogether, /'si:/. (In orthography, one may find *y'see* or *'see*.) Also, the phrase is normally spoken as a separate tone-unit, with a rising tone on *see*. (In rapid speech, there may be loudness alone.) This prosodic identity is usually required to avoid ambiguity with the other, literal use of *you see*, as in

(i) you |SÉE| I'm |quite HÀPPY here|
(ii) you |see I'm 'quite HÀPPY here|.

The second sentence means 'you are able to see' or 'you are aware' that the speaker is happy—a tag-question (e.g. *don't you*) might be attached; whereas the first means something like 'let me take you into my confidence . . . I'm quite happy here' (*don't you* would not be permissible). As with *you know*, this distinction is not always made in rapid speech, but the possibility for contrast is always present.

The intonation of this phrase tends to change from position to position. When initial, it is generally spoken in a higher pitch-range than the speaker's norm; medially, it is spoken within the average pitch-range; and finally, it is spoken within a low pitch-range, often integrated within the preceding tone-unit, as in the above example. The pitch of *you* is usually lower than that of *see* in all cases.

As in the other softening phrases, *you see* has a largely stylistic force. In initial position, it is essentially a request for a sympathetic hearing for whatever is to be said; the speaker wants to assure his listener that what follows is being said with the best of intentions, and that even if what is being said is unpleasant or forceful in some way, he wishes to soften the force of it in advance. Notice the difference between the following two sentences:

(i) there's another side to what you've been saying
(ii) you see, there's another side to what you've been saying.

The first is distinctly more abrupt and forceful than the second. To accompany the *you see*, the speaker may well make some kinesic gesture, such as leaning over and taking the other person's hand or arm (depending on how well they know each other). This sense merges with a more literal implication, whereby the listener is informed that the speaker has information which he needs to be told about, e.g. you |SÉE| |you can only 'stay for 'three WÈEKS|. However, it is very easy to give the impression of being condescending in this use, especially if the listener considers the information to be obvious, or unnecessary, and the foreigner must be careful not to use the phrase too casually.

Alternatively in initial position, it may be used simply as a kind of hesitation feature, indicating that what follows is to be an alternative point of view to what has already been put forward. In such cases, there is little clear difference between *you see* and *you know* used initially.

In medial and final positions, two functions of *you see* may be distinguished. Firstly, it acts as a summary to the point of the utterance so far—a 'pause' in which the speaker says 'if you've understood what I've been saying'. (As a result, overuse may be interpreted as being in effect an accusation of stupidity, and one should take care.) Secondly, it asks in effect for permission to continue the line of argument, by providing the listener with an opportunity to interrupt or respond. In final position it is usually followed by a pause, and acts as a signal that a response would be accepted; though often the speaker continues nonetheless.

Lastly, note the rather more insistent and formal use, *do you see*, possible in all positions, and also *don't you see*, though this is less common. Put in contrast, the various phrases show an increase in the amount of forcefulness with which the speaker is checking up on the comprehension of the listener:

(i)   they'll never allow us to go, you see;
(ii) they'll never allow us to go, do you see;
(iii) they'll never allow us to go, don't you see.

(iii) *I mean*
This phrase may be used initially, medially or finally in an utterance.
Initially, after a pause, as in

I |MÈAN| |what are we 'going to do NÒW|.

Medially, as in

the |people in the 'other HÒUSE| I |MÈAN| are |ÀLWAYS 'ready
to 'help|.

Finally, as in

|is there going to be ANÒTHER 'car 'there| I |MÉAN|.

In all positions the vowel of *I* tends to be reduced in quality,
producing /ə'miːn/; and sometimes it is so quietly articulated as to be
inaudible, /'miːn/. At normal conversational speed, there is no
obvious difference between *I mean* and *a mean*. Prosodic accuracy is
important, as with *you know* and *you see*, in order to ensure avoidance
of any confusion with the similar construction using *mean* as a full
verb. Compare, for example

(i) I |MÈAN| he |ought to 'buy a new CÀR|
(ii) I |mean he 'ought to 'buy a new CÀR|.

The first sentence means something like 'In other words...' or
'What I've been saying amounts to the following...'; the second
sentence means 'My specific meaning is that...' or 'I insist that...'.
In normal speed of speaking, the second sentence has a stronger
articulation of the pronoun, and the phrase is integrated within the
prosodic structure of the succeeding construction.

The meaning of this phrase is extraordinarily difficult to define:
it seems to perform a variety of semantic functions, some of which are
more important than others in any given instance. Generally speaking, its main function is to indicate that the speaker wishes to clarify
the meaning of his immediately preceding expression. This clarification may stem from a number of reasons and take a number of forms:
for example, the speaker may wish to restate his previous utterance
(e.g. because it is syntactically too awkward to complete as it stands,
or because he has chosen a wrong, careless, or ambiguous word);

or he may wish to provide some extra information or a fresh angle about the previous topic; or perhaps he simply wishes to change his mind. For example,

I |MÈAN| you |can't be'lieve a ↑THÌNG he says| he's a |DRÈAD-FUL 'liar|.

'I mean' provides a simple way of acheiving any of these aims, by giving the speaker the chance of simply stopping and starting again, or adding on some syntax to make the point clear. (In formal discourse, it would be necessary to develop more complex methods of incorporating such points, e.g. by the use of further subordinate clauses.)

Initially, the normal pitch movement is falling, as in the above examples. The phrase may however be used with a level tone (not usually with a rising tone, which would imply a literal meaning) and it may be followed by a pause, as in

I |MĒAN| – |what's the BÈST way of 'doing it|.

In initial or final positions, it may also be used with a falling tone, often after a pause, to express discontent, irritation or disapproval at a state of affairs, as in

you |can't 'do 'things like THÀT| – I |MÈAN|.

With a rising-falling tone, the implications are intensified. Alternatively, one might hear *I mean to say* in this position, where *say* is obligatorily nuclear.

It should be noted that in medial position, it may not always be clear which part of the sentence *I mean* is intended to replace; but ambiguity can be avoided by ensuring that the phrase is clearly linked intonationally to one part of the sentence or the other. In the example at the beginning of this section, for instance, if it is *the people in the house* which the speaker is using to replace something which occurred previously, then *I mean* will be attached to this and followed by a pause; alternatively, if it is *readiness to help* which is replacing something, the *I mean* will be attached to this, and preceded by a slight pause, the whole phrase being speeded up.

(iv) *sort of, kind of*

These phrases may be used immediately before any word or phrase about which there is uncertainty, vagueness, or idiosyncrasy, e.g.

it's |got a 'sort of ↑greenish 'blue RÒOF|.

They seem to be controlled solely by semantic factors: it is inappropriate to use them before clearly specific words, or words about which there could be no dispute as to meaning, e.g. *my |car has sort of FÒUR wheels| or *I |sort of ÀM 'hungry|. From the distributional point of view, they will be found to occur in almost any syntactic position within a sentence. They are not normally found in initial positions, i.e. as sentence connectors. They may, however, occur finally, in a low pitch range, as in

he |used to 'work as an ACCÒUNTANT 'sort of|,

but usually in this position the phrase is expanded to *sort of thing* or *kind of thing*. They may also occur in isolation, as in

A: |have you 'been on HŎLIDʌY| B: well |SÒRT ÓF|

It is normal to find *of* drawled and followed by a pause. In quick speech, *sort of* is pronounced /ˈsɔːtə/, and as speed increases, this tends to become /ˈsɔːrə/, and even /ˈsrə/; and a variant of /r/ is more likely to be heard in place of /t/ in American accents and 'r-coloured' varieties of British English. Likewise, /ˈkaɪndə/ tends to become /ˈkaɪnə/. *kind of* is used more frequently in America than in Britain; it is a vocalization learned early by children imitating American cowboys. Another point of pronunciation is that these phrases introduce the normal elision of /-v/ (in *of*) before consonants. (This is normal conversational practice, as can be seen from such phrases as 'cup of tea' /⁽ˡ⁾kʌpəˈtiː/ and the institutionalized form 'cuppa', or 'pint of milk' /ˈpaɪntəˈmɪlk/ and the recent form 'pinta', popularized by the television advertising jingle 'Drinka pinta milka day'.) The /-v/ of *of* is often (not invariably) used before a following vowel, as in 'sort of obvious' /⁽ˡ⁾sɔːtəvˈɒbvɪəs/.

(v) *mind you*

This phrase may be used medially or finally, and initially as a response within a discourse, as follows.
Initially, as in

|mind YÒU| I |think he has a PÒINT|.

Medially, as in

when|ever he CÒMES MÍND you| he's |always HELPFUL|.

Finally, as in

I |wouldn't be'lieve a 'word he SÀYS 'mind 'you|.

In all cases, there is assimilation between the two words, to produce /maɪnˈʤuː/—as if it were 'mine Jew'. Initially and medially, both words are normally spoken with equal prominence, displaying a parallel intonational movement, either falling, as in ⟍⟍ , or rising, as in ⟋⟋ . (Technically, the first tone is *subordinate* to the second in each case.) It is also common to hear reduced emphasis on *you*, producing ⟍• and ⟋° . In final position, it is uncommon to hear any intonational prominence at all, the phrase normally being fully incorporated within the intonational contour of the main tone-unit, usually as part of the 'tail' of that unit.

This is another phrase whose meaning is extremely difficult to delimit. We have noted a number of different 'strands' of meaning, of which the most important seems to be the expression of some kind of contradiction, with a reduced or apologetic force. The speaker feels the need to state a different or additional viewpoint from what he or other speakers have already expressed, but he wishes to do this without causing offence. It would be most unlikely to find this phrase being used in conjunction with threatening behaviour on the part of the speaker (e.g. *mind you, get out!*) In addition, *mind you* is used to express the speaker's awareness that he is (a) saying something controversial, and is worried about the possibility of being disagreed with later, or (b) saying something which he thinks is obvious, but which his listener may dispute. This 'defensive' meaning of the phrase is well illustrated in 10.71.

(vi) *yes* and *no*

Yes, used as a softener, is generally only found initially, with a rapid, clipped pronunciation, as in

yes I |think you òUGHT to come|.

The use of *yes* in such sentences is in effect to summarize a conviction built up over previous sentences, either on the part of the same speaker, or someone else. It is still an agreement-noise, but it is not necessarily an affirmation of the basic meaning of the sentence it follows; it rather indicates that the speaker agrees with a previously stated attitude. The clear pointer to this is to observe the use of *yes* in front of negative sentences, as in |yes he 'ought NÒT to a'pologize|. Here the affirmative value of the *yes* applies to the sentence as a whole; the speaker is indicating general agreement about the overall attitude being expressed. It is important to know that *yes* may be used in this way, in order to understand why there is really no contradiction when different speakers give opposite reactions to a sentence such as the above. After the sentence '*he ought not to apologize*', you may hear one person saying *yes* and the other person saying *no*. There is no necessary contradiction however: the first person is simply affirming the message of the sentence as a whole, i.e. 'you are right to say what you have said'; the second person is reinforcing the negative element within the sentence.

One may find *yes* introduced within a sentence, especially in utterances which are undergoing replanning by the speaker, as in

> there are two important points here and I think yes that you were right to deal with the local issue first . . .

One might hear *yes* inserted at almost any point within such utterances.

Also initially, one may hear *oh yes*, in the same sense as above.

No used as a softener has a very similar range of use to *yes*, but of course with the opposite semantic implications. It is generally used initially in sentences, the interesting point being that the sentence may have either a negative or a positive mood, as in

> no I |think he's ↑just the 'man for the JÒB|.

When it is used with the sense 'I agree with your negative interpretation', one may see the speaker *nodding* his head while simultaneously saying *no*. This has sometimes caused the foreign learner some surprise, but it is readily explicable if the distinction between verb-phrase negation and sentence negation is kept in mind.

(vii) *well*

The primary use of this word is initially in utterances within a discourse, as in 'well I |wouldn't quite say THĂT|'. In this position, however, it has three distinct pronunciations and meanings.

(a) It may be said slowly, drawled, usually with a falling-rising or rising tone, to imply such attitudes as reservation or doubt. The use means 'I'm sorry I have to say this, but . . .'

(b) It may be said in a rapid, clipped manner, in which case the attitude involved would be more business-like, implying that the speaker wishes to get on with his narrative. This may at times lead to an impression of abruptness, impatience, or something similar.

(c) Drawled with a level tone, it is simply an exponent of hesitation, indicating indecision, or, quite commonly, a casual or leisurely attitude on the part of the speaker, which he might be deliberately introducing in order to maintain the informality of a situation.

The word may also be introduced medially, as in

as he |CÀME ÍN| he · well |STÙMBLED I sup'pose you'd 'say| . . .

Here, usually the second pronunciation above would be used; but in hesitant speech one might hear either of the others.

The word is not used in final position.

Well usually occurs initially in any string of softening-phrases, as in *well mind you* . . ., *well you know* . . . If it occurs in second place, it is usually preceded by a brief pause, as in *yes · well* . . . or *I mean · well* . . ., and this usage would generally be considered hesitant. The normal pronunciation in strings is (b) above; the others would occur only if the string as a whole was given a slow articulation. *Well* may never co-occur with itself in any of its softening senses—*well well!* is an exclamation.

(viii) *but er*

The important thing to note about this phrase is its tendency to occur in final position in a sentence or discourse, as in

. . . so I |said I'd ↑see him on ↑TÙESDAY| |but er ·

Here the phrase functions as an indication that the speaker has finished what he wanted to say, and either does not want or is unable to say any more, but he is nonetheless aware that the subject-matter of the conversation has not been thoroughly or sufficiently expressed. It is an indication to the listener that while there is more to be said, the speaker himself is not anxious to continue. Of course if the listener does not want to continue the conversation either, there will be a pause, or an 'awkward silence', at the end of which someone might think up something to say about the same topic, or (more likely) there will be a change of subject-matter.

In order for this sense to be clear, the phrase must be said in a low pitch range. To increase pitch and loudness gives the reverse impression—that you are anxious to continue. The other prosodic characteristic which seems invariable is that the /t/ is lengthened, producing a hesitant or meditative effect.

This phrase also has an important additional use in initial position, where it expresses tentativeness or unwillingness to take up an opposite point of view from one listener, or to utter something that is likely to offend. One might well imagine a timid husband saying to

his overbearing wife: 'but er—you said I *could* go out this evening'!
An example of the 'awkward' initial use may be seen in 2.24.

As is clear from the extracts, softening connectives may be used in
combinations, the effect being to increase the overall impression of
tentativeness, hesitancy, informality, etc. With the exception of *well*,
there seem to be few restrictions on sequence. *well*, *yes* and *no* are
usually initial; and *mind you* also tends not to be used in second
position in a sequence. Apart from this, pairs of connectives may be
heard in any order. Sequences of more than two are possible, but
uncommon. However, as many as four may occur in succession, as in
the following example:

> yes well I mean you know you |can't ex'pect to 'get away with
> THĂT|.

Note that such sequences would be rapidly articulated if they occurred before the onset of the tone-unit.

In all cases, one should note the readiness of these connectives
to be used also in final positions in sentences. There is, however, a
difference in effect: in final position, the phrases generally take on a
'summarizing' force. Whereas initially they have a clearly reinforcing
function, often with the softening effect discussed above, which reduces the force of what is about to be said, in final position the
softening effect and the reinforcement is much less noticeable, and
the main function seems to be to indicate that the speaker is ready to
pause, and would tolerate an interruption. Indeed, in some cases—
especially with *you see* and *you know* and also with *I suppose* and *if
you like*—the phrases take on some literal meaning in final position,
almost like a question-tag. They are often heard after a considerable
pause, or repeated after the sentence to which they were originally
attached, as in:

> I'll |come 'home at ↑THRÈE if you LÍKE| – – – |if you LÍKE|

where the speaker has waited for a reaction from his listener, fails to
get one, and reintroduces his stimulus. Another clear example of this
process is in the use of *you know* and *I mean* reported above.

A further point to note concerning connective phrases is that they
must be pronounced as single lexical units, rhythmically and intonationally. They always have a unified prosodic shape, and in
unstressed syllables vowels are reduced in quality, as the examples

make clear. To speak these with equal prominence on each word produces highly disjointed and often unintelligible speech.

Other syntactic features of connectivity

We have space only for a brief discussion and illustration of the many other syntactic processes involved in connectivity, some of which have been referred to in our commentary on the extracts. We may group these under three main headings.

(i) *Ellipses*

Parts of the sentence whose meaning is obvious from the situation or verbal context are frequently omitted in conversational speech. (Cf. Quirk *et al.*, 1972: § 9.18, ff.).

(a) In particular, the Subject of the sentence tends to be omitted, as the following examples show: *says it costs him about the same amount* (1.27), *didn't really enjoy the flames very much* (2.14), *really does* (3.100), *hope you enjoy the programme, don't know how you do it.*
This is especially common with first and second person pronouns, and with 'empty' *it*; third person pronouns are generally elided only when the preceding context makes the meaning clear, e.g. *There's John. Looks well.* (See also 2.35, 59; 4.75; 10.63.)

(b) Often the verb phrase—usually the verb *to be*—is elided as well, e.g. *only a couple of pounds* (7.45), *no money* (12.16), *very interesting, three o'clock—time to go.*
When this happens, a following article may also be dropped, e.g. *When did I leave? Same time as usual, Nice piece of cake that, Brighton? Marvellous place, Lovely day!*

(c) The auxiliary verb may also be elided, along with the subject: *Have a nice meal* (1.25), *See Susie standing in the garden* (9.40), *Remember John Jones?, Got your paper I see, Want to know how?, Ever thought about leaving?, Raining again!, Always asking for trouble he is, That a fact?, That you?*
Or the auxiliary verb alone may be elided: *You heard the latest? You like the chocolate?*
There are other elisions to be found in the extracts; for instance, of the article (5.1; ?4.67); preposition (12.20).

(ii) *Word order variations*

Most of the variants here are to enable a word or phrase to be brought forward into a more emphatic or focused position. (Cf.

Quirk *et al.*, 1972, Chapter 14.). Examples are: *although staying there I enjoy it* (14.19), *dreadful sort of claustrophobic places they are* (14.23), *for children it's a great idea* (15.15), *the fireworks themselves we have a little store of* (2.17).

Often this involves the use of a pronoun in Subject position which is subsequently clarified by a 'tag statement', e.g. *they were terrible, the pigs* (4.2), *it was lovely, our one* (7.1), *they can swim, can't they, mice* (8.73).

(iii) *Blends*

A sentence begins with one construction but finishes with a different construction, there being some shared feature which has promoted the confusion, e.g. *this is something I usually spend one lesson arranging what they want to talk about* (10.74), *I think it's the money they're charging is one thing* (13.8).

(See also 3.68.) More restricted cases of the same kind of thing occur when there is lack of concord, e.g. *there was so many entrances* (1.59), *there's some lovely houses* (6.57), *they just had to put their dressing gown on* (7.14).

And an example of word order contrast plus broken concord is: *they still looked very small mice, this first litter* (8.31).

Other confusions emerge in variation in the choice of tenses (e.g. 1.101; 12.20), disjointed syntax (e.g. 7.32ff.; 10.95ff.), and general incompleteness (e.g. 4.62; 6.69; 7.12; 8.19; 12.9, 27; 13.22; etc.).

(iv) *Prosodic connectivity*

The fundamental organization of spoken discourse involves the use of prosodic features, whose importance for marking the basic functional units of conversation has been increasingly recognized in recent years, for instance in the case of statement vs. question, types of tag question, and relative clauses. Generally speaking, however, attention has been restricted to a small set of basic pitch tones and tunes, it usually being tacitly assumed that connected speech is produced by using these in sequence. To do so would however produce an extremely dull, non-fluent and badly structured kind of speech. Connected speech uses the whole range of prosodic features —pitch, loudness, speed, rhythm, pause—as well as various other 'paralinguistic' tones of voice (e.g. whisper, huskiness, resonance) to modulate the 'basic' tunes of English. Exactly how this is done is still a subject of enquiry, but three main functions of prosody in language are now generally recognized: as a means of communicating personal attitude or emotion; as a means of identifying a stylistic level; and as a means of expressing grammatical relations. The extracts provide copious examples of complex 'clusters' of prosodic effects that expound meanings under each of these three headings. Thus under attitude, we find examples of persuasiveness (1.45–6); disparagement (1.77, 117; 3.95–7); boredom (2.43–6); interest (3.3); strong feeling (2.21; 3.12–13, 38; 4.2–3); mock surprise (3.24–5); disapproval (3.63–4); etc., and the commentary cites many more instances. Prosodic markers of informality are also frequent and obvious, e.g. the use of laughter, variations in speed and rhythm, the use of mock accents (4.41), etc. But the most important effects, from the point of view of the present section, are those which impose a formal organization on the movement of discourse within and between speakers. Here the following functions turn up most often in the data:

(i) expression of parenthetic information (1.9–10, 67–8; 3.18–20, 60–1, 114–15; 6.28–31; 10.42; 13.37)

(ii) to make an antithetical point (1.19; 3.24–5, 47; 10.11, 84–5)

(iii) to mark a significant new topic or change of direction in a narrative (3.1, 15; 5.14–15, 18, 30; 6.1, 43–4; 8.14; 9.50; 13.23)

(iv) to mark increased emphasis (3.31–3, 35–6, 123–4; 8.28; 9.36; 10.47)

(v) to demarcate a quotation (3.84–5, 104–5; 9.42; 10.59–60; 12.9)

(vi) to indicate a lack of significance in the order of a set of items (9.24–5; 10.64)

Summary

Exactly why a speaker chooses to introduce one of these connective features into his speech, as opposed to nothing at all, is an extremely complex problem, which we do not investigate further here. There are many kinds of constraint, operating on the fluency of discourse, which indicate the extent of a speaker's semantic planning (or lack of it), and which also indicate awareness of and desire to control the stylistic level of the conversation. The notion of 'expressing a meaning in the most appropriate way' is a much simplified view of conversational interaction. If we examine any one focal utterance, analysing the reasons which have led it to be the shape it is will involve us in considering many variables, of which the most important seem to be the following: (a) our awareness of what we have said previously in the conversation (e.g. A realizes that he is contradicting himself, so he alters his sentence structure); (b) our awareness of our on-going non-linguistic communicative activity (e.g. A realizes that a point can be made more effectively by a gesture, so he alters his sentence, or leaves it unfinished); (c) our awareness of the other participants in the conversation—what they have previously said, how they are visually reacting, whether they are trying to interrupt, and so on; and (d) our awareness of any general situational constraints which might affect the form of the language (e.g. increased noise level outside which causes A to repeat or paraphrase). For other information about these variables, we refer the interested reader to the bibliography on p. 128.

B Intelligibility

Colloquial elision

One of the most striking features of the language contained in the extracts is its speed. It is a commonplace to note that learners of a foreign language always think it is being spoken rapidly, and to say that this is a false impression deriving from their unfamiliarity; but we must not assume that therefore speed of speaking causes no difficulty at all. On the contrary. There are often considerable changes introduced into one's pronunciation solely because of the flexibility and casualness of the informal conversational situation. Knowing what these are is an important stage in developing the receptive fluency referred to in the Introduction; and it is also important as a means of preserving intelligibility and developing natural conversational rhythms in speech production. Good intonation presupposes good rhythmic ability; and good rhythmic ability presupposes proper articulation of the vowel and consonant sequences constituting the syllables of connected speech. Failure to use the appropriate segmental pronunciation of words and phrases, therefore, can have repercussions over a wide area of linguistic structure.

Almost all manuals of pronunciation begin by studying the sounds of English in isolated words, and 'build up' sequences of sounds into acceptable connected speech patterns at a later stage. Each of the words used to illustrate sound contrasts is articulated in isolation, and consequently the syllables involved are likely to be pronounced with considerable emphasis. Care is taken to ensure that, for example, initial and final consonants are articulated clearly, or that vowels are given their full, stressed value. The student who then moves to the study of sounds in connected speech is immediately faced with a problem. He finds that many of the pronunciation rules he has learned for words in isolation have to be *un-learned* when the words are put together into sequences. He has to learn to leave certain sounds out in certain positions (what is usually referred to as *elision*), and he has to learn that adjacent sounds may affect each other to the extent of altering their 'basic' identity (*assimilation*). Of course there is a point in adopting the above pedagogical procedure, especially in a language learning course where written materials are central; but there still remains a considerable gap between the pronunciation of words and phrases in isolation and in connected speech, and this ought not to be underestimated. In this section, then, we look at some of the elisions which have occurred most frequently in our data, and which the foreigner is likely to encounter very soon on his contacting informal English. Some informal pronunciations, such as 'perhaps' spoken as 'praps', are noticed very quickly; what is often not noticed is that there are clear pronunciation principles under-lying the use of such forms as 'praps', and that they are operating on many other words in the language besides. We have divided the elisions into two types: elisions within lexical items when used in colloquial speech, and elisions within specified grammatical struc-tures, when spoken colloquially.

Lexical elision

(a) *Vowels.* In polysyllabic words, one syllable is usually more prominent than all the others, and this we refer to as the *accented* syllable. In informal speech, the weak vowels (ə, ı and ʊ) of the unstressed syllables preceding and following this syllable in certain cases elide, and this has a considerable effect on the rhythm of the words as wholes.

(i) syllables after the accent tend to drop their weak vowels if these are unstressed and occurring between consonants, e.g. *probably* /'prɒblı/, *university* /juːnı'vɜːstı/, *difficult* /'difklt/. This is especially so if the consonant following is /r/ or /l/, as in *preferable* /'prefrəbl/, *ordinary* /'ɔːdnrı/, *different* /'dıfrnt/, *factory* /'fæktrı/, *family* /'fæmlı/, carefully /'kɛəflı/.

(ii) syllables before the accent, if they are unstressed, tend to drop their weak vowels, as in *police* /pliːs/, *suppose* /spəʊz/, *balloon* /bluːn/ and *perhaps* /præps/—the latter replacing the abnormal /ph-/ combination which would have emerged, with a more familiar combination /pr-/. In writing that attempts to reflect informal speech, these elisions are often represented by apostrophes, as in *op'ra*, *temp'ry*, or *s'pose*. One should note, also, that the range of elisions in (i) above applies only to British English. In American pronunciation, for instance, the stress patterns of many of these words is different, and the weak vowels are often retained—especially in words such as *temporary, category*.

(b) *Consonants*. The general tendency here is for consonant clusters to simplify in informal connected speech. This is especially the case with /t/ or /d/ between consonants, which tend to be omitted, as in *facts* /fæks/, *mostly* /'məʊslɪ/, *friendship* /'frenʃɪp/ and *dramatists* /'dræmətɪs/. The final -*s* is often long, /ss/. Front fricatives tend to elide before similarly articulated consonants, e.g. *clothes* becomes /kləʊz/. /l/ is commonly dropped when following a back mid-open vowel, as in *already* /ɔː'redɪ/. And there are a few other common elisions, such as *asked* /aːst/ and *recognized* /'rekənaɪzd/.

Grammatical elision

Here the tendency is to elide the vowels of grammatical words, which are often monosyllabic, and usually in an unstressed position in a sentence. Articles, conjunctions, pronouns, some prepositions, auxiliary verbs, and a few adverbial elements (such as introductory *there* in 'there is', etc.) are particularly affected. Examples are: *an* > /n/, *the* > /θ/, *and* > /n/, *but* > /bt/ (often with a devoiced [b̥]), *she* > /ʃ/, *some* > /sm/, *from* > /frm/, *can* > /kn/, *there are* > /ðəː/, and so on. Examples in sentences are:

there are lots of them /ðəː 'lɒts ə ðm/ or /ðəː'lɒtsvm/
she said the boys and girls can come /ʃ'sedð'bɔɪzŋ'gɜːlzkŋ'kʌm/

Of particular importance for comprehension is to realize that sequences of unstressed grammatical words may all be affected by this process of elision; and along with the assimilations which may follow due to the consonants being juxtaposed, the resulting speech may sound quite unlike its written form. This is particularly noticeable in verb phrases, with sequences of auxiliary verbs, as in *he wouldn't have been able to go*, which may regularly be heard /ɪ'wʊdnəbɪn 'eɪblə 'gəʊ/. This pronunciation is arrived at in the following way: the strong vowels of *have* and *been* get reduced; initial *h* is dropped in unstressed syllables; /t/ elides readily, as do front fricatives (/v/ in this case), as we have seen above—and the result is the pronunciation as transcribed. Other examples may be heard in

it'll have been five years /ɪtləbɪn 'faɪv 'jɪəz/
I should have told him /aɪʃd̥ə'təʊldɪm/
they shouldn't be here /ðeɪ 'ʃəmbɪ 'hɪə/.

C Appropriateness

Intelligibility and fluency, as we have pointed out, should be placed high among the aims of foreign learners who wish to do more than simply 'get by' in their command of conversational English, since to sound intelligible is essential, and to sound fluent is highly desirable, if anything approaching a 'real' conversational interchange is to take place between a foreign learner and a native English speaker. But there is something else that is of the greatest importance in ensuring successful conversational contact—appropriateness. The language used by many foreigners is completely intelligible, and attains quite a remarkable degree of fluency, but often fails to reach comparable standards of appropriateness in the conversational situation; and whereas native speakers will often go to great lengths to make allowances for shortcomings in the first two qualities—recognizing them as presenting real linguistic difficulties—they may be less able to make corresponding allowances for lapses in appropriateness, and may regard the use of an inappropriate grammatical pattern, intonation tune, or item of vocabulary as being evidence of a personal or psychological fault in the speaker rather than of a failure to cope with a genuine linguistic difficulty. This situation may be compared with that which we noted as regards mistakes of intonation (see p. 8 above).

To give a full account of what is meant by 'appropriateness' is beyond the scope of this—and perhaps any other—book: it would involve an exhaustive treatment of a wide range of linguistic features, and—even more formidable—an account of the relationship between those features and specific situations, since appropriateness must always be analysed in relation to some situation. However, this state of affairs should not be seized upon as an excuse for refusing to say anything at all about appropriateness: what we have done is to assume that there is at least an element of homogeneity in all situations that may be regarded as 'conversational' in our terms and then to deal mainly with that aspect of language in which the problem of appropriateness presents itself most acutely: the choice of vocabulary.[1] It is well known that colloquial language has its own distinctive lexis—such as *kids* (1.120), *quid* (1.78)—but there has been little

---

1. One should note in passing that syntactic features of informality are common in the extracts, e.g. *try and make* (10.10); *you* (for *one*) (10.14); neologistic formations, e.g. *spacecrafts* (2.31); B finishing off A's construction (1.82); loosely connected adjectives (1.26–7). They are not further discussed here.

attempt to distinguish patterns or types within the general notion. What we wish to do is to examine the lexis used in several of our extracts in some detail, calling attention to a number of ways in which the participants, as native speakers, successfully meet the requirements of conversational appropriateness, and on the basis of this examination to set up a few functional and formal categories that will suggest a means of approaching the bewildering mass of the colloquial vocabulary.

It is important that the categories should not be regarded as either the only possible ones, or even as adequately covering the field of colloquial vocabulary; but it seems to us that for pedagogical purposes some kind of ordering—however rudimentary—is preferable to simple alphabetic listing. In the notes to the extracts printed in Chapter 2, we have already pointed out a number of items of colloquial vocabulary: one way of extending a learner's knowledge of such items is to call attention to words and phrases which are formally or semantically related to them, or to quite different words which may be used for roughly similar purposes, and we make some suggestions of this nature in Chapter 4. Taking the process further, it is possible to gather vocabulary of this kind into ad hoc categories, which may be very different from each other, and determined simply on grounds of convenience, or interest, as a means of grouping items together in the hope of making them easier to remember, and again we have given examples of the process in Chapter 4.

In the notes it will have been seen that we pay attention not simply to colloquial lexical items as such, but also to habits of colloquial lexical behaviour: in addition to using an appropriate proportion of colloquial words and phrases, a speaker may maintain an impression of colloquial informality by the *way* in which he uses words which would normally be regarded as belonging to the standard vocabulary. Both of these aspects—the colloquial vocabulary per se, and typical colloquial lexical habits—receive attention in the rest of this section, where we consider imprecision, intensification and neologism.

Imprecision

Lack of precision is one of the most important features of the vocabulary of informal conversation, and it is well represented in the extracts. In informal situations, of course, a deliberate use of lexical vagueness is not necessarily something to be criticized. A perfectly succinct, precise, specific, controlled contribution to a conversation is the aim of many people participating in debates, discussions, interviews, and so on; but on informal occasions, this amount of intellectual control is often absent. The use of lexical vagueness is undoubtedly a main sign of social and personal relaxation; and while one would not normally expect to find someone consciously cultivating imprecision, the point must be firmly made that vague usage should not be avoided 'at all costs'; the foreign learner must be prepared to encounter a great deal of unfamiliar lexis as a result.

There are many reasons for lexical vagueness. In our opinion, the four most important are: (a) memory loss—the speaker forgets a word, or it may be 'on the tip of his tongue'; (b) there is no word in the language for what he wants to say, or he does not know the appropriate word; (c) the subject of the conversation is not such that it requires precision, and an approximation or characterization will do; and (d) the 'choice' of the vague lexical item is conducive to maintaining the informal atmosphere of the situation (where the use of a precise, formal word might jar). Any one instance of lexical vagueness may stem from any or all of these factors, of course, and it is sometimes difficult to distinguish them. There are, in addition‘ other likely factors (such as personal habit—cf. B's use of *etcetera* in Extract 6—or lack of control due to emotional involvement in the conversation); but we are in no way trying to establish a final classification here.

The way in which almost all of the speakers in our extracts tend to avoid an excess of precision for a good deal of the time may be seen clearly from the following instances, which are all drawn from the first five extracts—many more are to be found in the rest of the material: *something like that* (3.27), *or something* (3.86), *some, somewhere* (3.114; 4.25); *probably* (3.31, 49); *in a way* (3.65); *apparently* (4.12; 5.46); *it didn't matter where it was* (4.67).

It is possible to discern distinct types of lexical vagueness within the general spectrum of imprecision that one finds in conversational English. At one extreme we find a range of lexical items which express *total* vagueness. Here, the intended lexical item is not available to the speaker, for whatever reason, and he therefore substitutes an item which indicates that it is not available, as is the case with *things* (1.16). English has a number of items which seem to have evolved specifically to fulfil this function. Their spelling is somewhat uncertain, since they are features of the spoken language only, and they include *thingummy* /'θɪŋəmɪ/, *thingy* /'θɪŋɪ/, *thingummajig* /'θɪŋəmə-ʤɪg/, *thingummabob* /'θɪŋəmɪbɒb/, *whatsisname* /'wɒtsɪzneɪm/, *whatsit(s)* /'wɒtsɪt(s)/, *what-do-you-call-it* /'wɒtʃʊkɔːlɪt/ or /'wɒtʃəməkɔː-

lıt/ (the latter presumably from an earlier 'what you may call it'), *oojamaflip* /'uːʤəməflıp/, *doo-da* /'duːdaː/. In sentences, one might hear *Pass me the whatsit(s), will you?, I gave the book to thingummy in the corner-shop*, and so on.

Another type of vagueness occurs at the end of a sequence of lexical items (such as a list), where completion in specific terms is unnecessary. Here one might simply use a summarizing phrase, such as *and things* (2.60), *and things like this* (2.32), *and the like, and so on* (10.7), *and so on and so forth, and so forth, and everything* (1.18, 31: 6.16, 33), *the whole thing* (10.11), *something* (14.4), *etcetera* (6.7 etc.), and the common *sort of thing*. For example, in response to a casual enquiry about what you have in your shopping basket, it would not normally be appropriate to go through the entire contents, giving a precise inventory; a general indication of the content, followed by a summarizing phrase, would do, as in *I've got some tomatoes, beans, and things*.

Also tied to particular grammatical structures we find the use of vague generic terms and collective nouns, such as *bags of, stacks of, tons of, heaps of, oodles of, umpteen*, and *a touch of*. Examples: *I've got bags of time, He's got oodles of money, I think I've got a touch of my hay-fever coming on*. All of these phrases except the last mean simply 'lots of'; the last means 'an instance of'. Tied to a negative structure, we find *for anything*, as in *I wouldn't have his job for anything*, along with such other phrases as *for worlds, for the world, for all the tea in China*. At this point, we are getting close to the imprecision that is associated with intensification or unduly vivid description— also found very widely in the extracts; but this in itself is so important a feature of colloquial vocabulary that we treat it as a separate category.

Before leaving the matter of imprecision, it is worth mentioning the wide range of devices that the colloquial lexicon contains which allows for approximations to be made. Approximate numbers or quantities are particularly important, and with *a class of thirty odd* (10.72) may be compared: *there were about/round about thirty in the class, there were getting on for thirty, there were thirty give or take a couple, thirty as near as makes no difference, thirty as near as dammit*. Compare also: *he was a shade under/over six feet tall, she was getting on for/knocking on (for) forty*. And as far as various qualities are concerned, it is worth noting the extreme flexibility of the 'approximating' suffix *-ish*, which may be attached to a wide range of nouns and adjectives, to give, for instance, *mannish, womanish, boyish,* *tallish, shortish, fattish, thinnish, fortyish, whitish, purpleish*, and so on. A similar effect may be obtained by means of the phrase *sort of* (cf. p. 99 above).

Intensification

Under this heading we include a number of features which we have found to be very characteristic of conversation. Foremost among these is the tendency towards exaggeration. The underlying intention is almost invariably humorous—to hear someone genuinely exaggerating is rather tiresome, and usually leads to them being regarded as a bore; but rhetorical exaggeration is a useful means of engaging the listener's interest, giving the speaker greater scope for self-expression and also of maintaining the informality of a conversational situation. Looking again no further than our first five extracts, it is possible to find the following assortment of exaggerative devices: *huge* (2.7); *absolutely infuriating* (3.13); *absolutely perfectly* (5.42); *horrible* (3.53); *tremendous* (3.123); *furious* (4.14); *passionately fond of* (4.61); *terrible* (5.1); *horrifying* (5.1); *slapped on* (5.18); *frantically* (5.19); *shaking like a leaf* (5.35); *terrifying* (5.39); *with the utmost deliberation* (5.41); *collapsed* (5.47); *state of hysteria* (5.47); and, a very striking example, *dirty shuffling monsters in acres of mud* (4.71).

A second type of intensification is by the use of items, typically adjectives and adverbs, which are introduced as a general means of expressing emotional emphasis in a semantically non-specific way. It has often been noted that some of these items are restricted to particular social groups, and may come into and go out of fashion relatively rapidly. Adjectives of this kind include: *fantastic* (1.87); *marvellous* (4.10, 24); *wonderful* (4.10); and *super* (14.5). To these might be added; *smashing, perfect, superb, beautiful, gorgeous*, and *great*. As these examples suggest, such items tend to be markers of approval, but expressions of negative attitude can be found, e.g. *grotty, yucky*.

Another example is the set of adverbs which are freely used in colloquial conversational English to modify the meaning of adjectives and other adverbs: *absolutely* (3.13, 4.7, 17); *perfectly* (3.117, 118); *rather* (6.26); *all* (1.30, 2.10, and cf. 2.31); *a bit* (2.5, 4.75); *really* (4.28); *pretty* (5.38). All these instances may be seen as intensifying the effect of the items they modify, and to them we should add at least *bloody*, as perhaps the commonest impolite adverbial intensifier, *just*, and *jolly*. A more detailed classification of these items may be found in Quirk *et al.*, Chapter 8, where in particular there is a discussion of other words whose effect is to soften, rather than intensify the adjective or adverb to which they are attached, for instance *quite* (3.24. See the discussion of 'downtoners' in Quirk *et al.*, § 8.29ff.). Grammatically, the kind of modification we have just been discussing is a feature of the noun phrase; but colloquial English also makes a great deal of use of a relatively small group of adverbs— for instance *actually* (3.30, 112); *obviously* (3.70, 122); *just* (1.31)—to perform the functions of intensifying and softening at the level of clause, or sentence. But such items are really to be considered from a syntactic, rather than lexical point of view, and so we do not treat them in detail here. (But see pp. 90–1 above.)

Although these types of lexis illustrate what seem to be the main tendencies, they do not exhaust all that might be included under the heading of intensification. As far as grammar is concerned, for example, we have already made a brief reference to the variations of word order which add extra emphasis (p. 104 above). In addition, a very frequent feature of the extracts is the use of prosodic means of intensifying lexical meaning, in particular by lengthening a sound or syllable, as in: *breezy* (1.28); *boring* (1.30); *big* (2.9); *absolutely* (3.12); *beginning* (3.17); *vicious* (3.38); *crunching* (5.18); *reasonably* (6.35); *extravagant—extraordinarily—expensive* (6.37); *off* (8.63); *swore* (9.36).

Neologism

Lastly, an important process is the way the native speaker readily constructs new lexical items—or *neologisms*—to meet the needs of a particular occasion. By 'new' here, we mean fresh coinages, words made up on the spur of the moment, which are in no dictionary, and which may never be used again. They are sometimes called 'nonce-words'—that is, words made up 'for the nonce' (as Elizabethan English would have put it), for a single occasion of use. The extracts show a few examples of this, as in *sparkly* (2.29); *half-like* (14.12); and *open-ended* (10.26), though this last is not so much a new word as a new sense for a familiar word. Clearly, nonce-usage is similar to the linguistic creativity found in humour, or in the use of figurative language, as when B talks about a *sprinkling* of shops in 6.36. It is at the opposite end of the scale from the items grouped together under the heading of exaggeration, which are for the most part conventional expressions, and in many cases verging on cliché. There are in fact many instances in the extracts where conventional senses are being modified or stretched beyond normally recognized dictionary meanings, e.g. *indulge* (2.2); *store* (2.17); *east and west* (6.68); *arena* (8.6); *immaculate conception* (8.15). The use of affixes is a main means of extending the vocabulary in a neologistic way. Prefixes such as *semi-*, *multi-*, and *non-*, and suffixes such as *-like*, and *-wise* are frequently used to express approximation, when precision is not of primary concern. We may cite such examples as *That mountain is rather table-like, isn't it*, which is a more informal version of *like a table*, or *Linguistics-wise I think she's quite clever*, where one is avoiding the cumbersomeness of a circumlocution such as *From the point of view of linguistics* . . . Native speakers manipulate their language in this way all the time in informal speech. To our mind, it is the mark of a real command of a foreign language when the learner dares to do likewise.

4

Teaching Implications

In the Introduction to this book, we laid a great deal of emphasis on the notion that informal conversational English presents a rather different kind of language from that which many foreign learners will be accustomed to hearing in their classrooms or on tape. As a result of this, the teacher is likely to find himself faced with a number of difficulties, peculiar to this variety of English. We hope, then, that by being aware of the main sources of difficulty in using material of this kind, some of the more awkward pedagogical problems will be anticipated, and their effect minimized.

The biggest problem will be to get the students acclimatized to this kind of English. Most students will have spent the whole of their English-speaking lifetime in contact with relatively formal varieties of the language—the language of radio, film documentary, the classroom, and other places where care and precision are generally expected. They will therefore find informal conversational English something of a surprise, and are likely to react to it with some such judgment as 'ungrammatical', 'lacking rules' or 'impure'. This is an understandable reaction, but one which must be quickly and firmly put in perspective. The teacher must strongly emphasize the normality of this kind of English, and reassure his students that these features, which are unfamiliar in many other kinds of English—especially in writing—are precisely what give to informal conversation its main stylistic character, and ought not to be apologized for. He must go into the characteristics of the social situations which have given rise to these extracts, and make it clear that the success of the conversation is largely due to the linguistic features of informality, some of which have been discussed in the analysis section of this book. The participants feel they are communicating satisfactorily—which means not only getting their meaning across to each other but also maintaining the social atmosphere they feel to be appropriate to the occasion. The language of these extracts, therefore, must be accepted, and not criticized; but developing new perspectives of acceptability will take time. To help matters, the teacher might make the point that there are both native and non-native 'mistakes' which the student will encounter, and that whereas the latter are to be eliminated, as far as possible, the former should be seen as an important part of a natural colloquial style. If necessary, one could take examples from the student's own language, showing that there are characteristics there similar to those being studied in English. It would be important, too, to explain why there is such a difference between much conventional teaching material and 'real' conversation—in particular, the difficulty of obtaining good samples of genuine 'everyday conversation', and the problems involved in devising a useful system of transcription for such matters as intonation and rhythm. Also, students could be reminded of how the history of English language study has been so taken up with written forms of the language, and how it is only recently that the primacy of the spoken language has come to be widely recognized. It is to be expected, then, that some students will react against the language of the extracts, because it is not what they are used to, and not what they have been taught to use. Our reaction to this, accordingly, is to stress that if there are to be linguistic shocks of this kind, it is far better to encounter these in the classroom than in real life. Early familiarity with informal English will minimize the risk of massive unintelligibility in everyday situations later, when the student arrives in an English-speaking situation. The sooner he comes to terms with informal conversation, and tries to master it, the better.

One point should be made very clearly before a student tries to work systematically through the material in this book. When we say 'tries to master it', we are not suggesting that all the characteristics of informal English should be introduced into the classroom as part of the *productive* use of language on the part of the student. On the contrary. The main aim of this book is to put the student in contact with a wide range of English usage, in order to improve his discrimination and comprehension of the language. To take the extreme case, which could arise out of a consideration of some of the above extracts, there is no point whatsoever in *teaching* students to be non-fluent, hesitate, or make mistakes in an English kind of way; but it is essential that they be taught how to interpret the speech of native speakers which *will* contain such 'errors'. Likewise, if a student has already habituated himself to a particular grammatical pattern which happens to belong to a more formal kind of English than that studied here, it would be retrograde to attempt to impose the informal pattern on him in any rigorous, explicit way. The student would find himself suddenly faced with the need to control a large number of alternatives between formal and informal variants, would lack the time to process these in normal speech-situations, and as a result might end up speaking a far less fluent kind of English than would otherwise be the case. Worse, this would very likely be an inconsistent amalgam of structures and pronunciations from different styles, some formal, some informal. The policy we advocate, therefore, is one of exposure: the student should be allowed to come into contact with as much informal English as possible. In the course of time, some of the features of this will rub off onto the student, and he may begin to develop a command of informal expression himself. This process, we believe, can be speeded up by an analytic concentration in class on the main points of difference, supplemented by selective and judicious practical work. It is this belief which has led to the present book. But at all times, the approach for the advanced learner should be flexible and gradual, and should emphasize the development of receptive skills before productive ones.

However, we do not wish to make too bold a distinction between receptive and productive abilities. We are aware, for instance, that improvement in articulatory skills can assist the development of discrimination ability and comprehension; and that consequently it may at times prove useful to allow the student to introduce 'new' linguistic features into his speech, even if they are at variance with features he has already learned. This will be particularly useful, for example, when he comes into contact with regional dialects and accents; but it is a principle which applies to syntax too. Moreover, the teacher must be ready to introduce the features of informal conversation into the student's production if an opportunity arises. To go back to the example of non-fluency, if students do find themselves in a state of hesitation (which is reasonably likely!), then they should be able to express this in an English way, making the conventional self-corrections and hesitation noises (with appropriate vowel-qualities) in order to preserve the continuity of their utterance; but for this, some practice would undoubtedly be necessary. Above all, the need to soak the student in the normal rhythms and intonations of everyday speech (as opposed to the prosody of formal English, or of written English read aloud, which so often is what has previously been given) requires an attack on both fronts, receptive and productive.

It would seem to follow from what has been said, of course, that the earlier any exposure to conversational English takes place, the better. We see no reason why the most junior of classes should not be exposed to a little informal English at regular intervals right from the beginning of their English-learning career. It would not be necessary for the beginners to understand all, or even most of the language used; the aim would be to present them with prosodically normal, fluent utterance, to give them a feeling for the norms of intonation, speed, loudness and rhythm of English pronunciation, for the voice quality of a British speaker (or an American one, as the case may be), all of which may be considerably different from their own. The emphasis on connected speech (especially in dialogue) which this would bring could have a marked effect on their rhythmic production, and would, of course, make for a continuity of development between the early years and the more 'advanced' ones. Students reared on such material would hardly be likely to display the attitudes of shock mentioned earlier. If this were regularly done in schools, it goes without saying that our book, with its present emphasis, could no longer be realistically labelled as 'advanced'!

A further point to bear in mind in evaluating informal English for classroom use is that the data subsumed under this heading in fact present varying amounts of informality. Informal features of language may be found at all levels of organization, as we have seen— in pronunciation (both segmental and prosodic), in grammar, and in vocabulary. And it is quite normal to find kinds of informal English which make use of these levels in different combinations. For example, an otherwise 'neutral' kind of English may be made slightly informal by an occasional introduction of colloquial vocabulary; adding some informal syntax would make the overall speech more informal; and so on. And, if all three levels are involved, it is possible to find speakers who use but a small range of informal features very frequently, and others who use a wide range of such features, but less frequently. In short, English presents many kinds and degrees of informality. The student must be prepared for this, and accept it, in much the same way as he must be prepared to meet people of varying personalities in everyday life. He must also try to develop an intuitive awareness of the amount of informality in a conversation. After all, a clear measure of his control of English culture-patterns will be the extent to which he can assess the amount of formality required or tolerated in a communication situation, and choose the appropriate range of expression for it. A view of English, then, which sees informality as a rigid homogeneous system of rules is as far from the truth as a view of the language which sees only formality there.

Finally, in selecting points for commentary in this material, we have tried to deal with points of pronunciation, syntax and vocabulary which have on the whole been ignored or minimized in the standard approaches. Thus one will find in these pages a rather greater emphasis than normal in language-teaching courses being given to such matters as intonation and stylistic effect. Again, there is a great deal of information about connected speech, which our extracts provide, which we do not know to be available elsewhere. As a result, we have not paid much attention to the more well-recognized problems of English. Tag-questions, for example, are just as 'advanced' a problem, in many ways, as the matters discussed in this book; but because there are so many standard discussions of tags in the English Language Teaching literature, we have not gone systematically into the matter here. The teacher, then, should check— especially before proceeding to the analytic sections of this book— that the general vocabulary and the more elementary grammatical aspects of the extracts *are* in fact understood by the student. Unless this is done, there is always a danger of his being unable to concentrate on the syntactic or phonological issues dealt with in the analysis because of some unconnected difficulty. Also, as a general check, the teacher ought to ascertain that the extracts have been generally understood, using conventional techniques of comprehension testing.

Extending the approach

We do not propose to enter into an exhaustive discussion of the kinds of teaching procedure which these materials might suggest, as our purpose is more to provide source materials for others to experiment with. There are however various ways in which the materials presented in this book can be used as a basis for extending the student's ability in and knowledge of English, and we list some which we have found to be most useful.

1. Specific exercises in listening accuracy and comprehension can readily be devised using the taped material, focusing on points of difficult interpretation due to oddly inverted syntax, rapid pronunciation, marked intonational emphasis, and so on. As this is the most obvious and well-established way in which material of this kind might be used, we do not propose to illustrate it further here.

2. We have found that the extracts readily suggest areas for further

investigations of a linguistic or cultural kind. It is important to have some ancillary material available, especially whenever the extract is dealing with a topic that is relatively domestic or parochial in character. Under the linguistic heading, for example, one might aim to build up lexical sets within the same stylistic range. The colloquial vocabulary of the extracts can to a considerable degree be grouped into semantic types, and it makes an interesting exercise to indicate what these are and gather further examples from within the same areas, using dictionaries of colloquial English, modern drama texts, native speaker informants, and so on. Examples of such types would be: labels for individuals or social groups, e.g. *chap* (1.7; 5.3) (cf. *bloke, geezer, guy* ,etc.), *kids* (1.120; 4.15, 20) (cf. *nippers, youngsters, brood,* etc.); *skinheads* (3.15, 40, 42), *teddy boys* (3.45), *Pakis* (3.39); agreement formulae, e.g. *that's a point* (2.42), *there you are you see* (3.107), *really* (4.2), *quite* (4.34), *that's right* (4.43); time or place expressions, e.g. *every now and again* (1.44), *years ago* (5.3), *down the road* (1.3), *back in the Midlands* (2.46); terms for quantities, e.g. *couple* (2.30; 3.43), *bob* (1.24), *quid* (1.78); abbreviations (easily recognizable in writing, but often quite obscure in speech), e.g. *AA* (= Automobile Association); exclamations and expletives, e.g. *good Lord* (1.21), *blimey* (5.51), *ooh* (1.125). Suggestions for lexical sets within a more general cultural perspective would be: names of English football teams (arising out of Extract 1), further informal vocabulary for fireworks (Extract 2), other instances of rhyming slang (Extract 3), institutionalized names of animals (Extract 4), types of thoroughfare (Extract 6), types of school and related vocabulary (Extract 10). Here is an example of the kind of further lexical and cultural illustration we have in mind.

In Extract 10, a great deal of knowledge about school and school life is presupposed. This extract could therefore lead to a discussion of the British educational system, or its American counterpart. The relationship between the various educational stages might be represented diagrammatically, as follows:

The British System

PRIMARY			SECONDARY	
(nursery) — infant — junior			comprehensive ⟶ grammar ⟶ secondary modern	
3–4 yrs 5 7			11 16 18	

Discussion of the various stages would bring out such information as the following. *Nursery* schools are allowed for in the State educational system, but are not always provided. Attendance at them is not compulsory, since it is at the age of five that children legally have to start school. The *infant* and *junior* schools are in many cases housed in the same building, and may be regarded as departments within a single primary school. In other cases they may be separate schools. *Grammar* schools and *secondary modern* schools are the two halves of the traditional, selective system of education, in which pupils were selected for the grammar school if they passed an examination at the age of eleven (the 'eleven plus'), those who failed having to attend a secondary modern school. This system is gradually being replaced by a non-selective system of secondary education in which all pupils move at the end of primary schooling direct to a *comprehensive* school.

The American system:

	ELEMENTARY		SECONDARY	
primary —	grammar —	junior high —	high school	
5–6 yrs	8	12	14	18

The age of starting school in America may vary slightly from State to State, and is not fixed on a national basis as in Britain. *Elementary* school lasts until the age of 14, but note that the last two years are known as *junior high school*. It is also important to note the different applications of the terms *primary* and *grammar* between the two systems, British and American.

Moving on from here, the phrase *second form* (10.72) would provide an opportunity to talk about the internal organization of schools. *Form* here means 'class'; the older the pupils, the higher the form number (third form, fourth form, etc.). The corresponding American word is *grade*. School children tend to abbreviate, e.g. 'the fourth form' becomes 'the fourth'. If the numbers in any one year are large enough, or perhaps depending on academic ability, there may be divisions into separate classes, e.g. *upper fourth, lower fourth, 4A, 4B,* etc. The term *lower sixth*, however, normally refers to the first year of sixth form work, *upper sixth* to the second year. In secondary schools, the first important examination is usually taken in the fifth form, when most pupils are approximately 15–16 years old. This examination, the General Certificate of Education (generally referred to as the 'G.C.E.' /'dʒiː siː 'iː/), is increasingly being supplemented by another examination, the Certificate of Secondary Education (or C.S.E. /'siː es 'iː/), which was originally developed for use in schools which were not at one time equipped to provide teaching up to the standard required for G.C.E. After having passed the appropriate subject examinations at the level of G.C.E., pupils in grammar or comprehensive schools may then continue their education for a further two or more years in the sixth form, where they take their second important examination, the *Advanced Level* of the G.C.E. (usually referred to as 'A level' /'eɪ‚ levl/, opposed to the *Ordinary Level*, or 'O level' /'əʊ‚levl/ of the examinations taken earlier). At the present time, this is the standard qualifying examination for entrance to university in Britain and to a number of jobs and professions. It is worth noting that when 'pupils' proceed beyond secondary schooling to some branch of higher education, they are then referred to as 'students'.

As a final example of this process of cultural extension of the material, we might take the mention of *debate*, in 10.74, which follows on from the above. Here one might introduce a little of formal debating procedure. A *motion* (i.e. a formal proposal to be discussed) is *proposed* or *put forward* by one speaker, who delivers a speech in support of it. An example of a motion would be 'This house (i.e. the assembly present for the debate) believes that English teachers should be paid more'. The motion is then *opposed* by another speaker, who *speaks against* it. Each of these speakers is in turn supported by another, who *seconds* the opening speeches. The motion is then *open* for general discussion from *the floor* (i.e. members of the audience). At the end of the open discussion, the proposer and opposer *sum up* for and against the motion respectively. There is then a vote, and the motion is either *carried* or *defeated* (or *lost*).

3. It is difficult to devise exercises for the development of productive ability in colloquial speech without introducing a contradiction between the maintenance of structured drills and an appearance of spontaneous informality. Certain aspects of the material can however be used in productive exercises. In phonology, it is possible to practise degrees of reduction in the use of unstressed syllables, along with the appropriate range of assimilations and elisions. A range of linking forms can be practised in their weak and strong forms (e.g. |John CÁME| and |Mary LÈFT| vs. |John CÁME| |ĂND| |Mary LÈFT|). Comment clauses in particular need accurate

intonational and speed articulation. The teacher must point out to the student the reduced quality of the pronouns in *you know*, *I mean*, and *you see*. He has to correct students who try to give the full diphthongal quality to the *I*, or who start with too open a vowel; or who attempt to make a fully rounded /uː/ in *you*, or fail to produce the fairly clipped vowel of the second word in each phrase. He should remind them that if these pronunciation modifications are not made, the phrases will sound like their literal equivalents, and there may be ambiguity or unintelligibility, as in the examples on p. 92. However, if the teacher does decide to introduce these phrases in a systematic way, it must not be forgotten that with all such features, overuse is misuse. Too frequent a use of any grammatical pattern gives rise to boredom, irritability, and other like reactions on the part of a listener. Non-fluent English speakers are particularly prone to over-use softening phrases, in fact—introducing a 'sort of' or a 'you know' before almost every word. Some speakers have even assumed this as an affectation, and it has often been satirized as the mark of an uneducated aristocrat! The use of these features on occasions where fluency is expected (as in debate or in serious discussion) is also rightly criticized, as on the whole they are features indicating spontaneous, on-going linguistic construction in a pressure-free situation, and they are thus inappropriate in situations where it is assumed that clear thinking is the norm, and care has been taken to ensure precision and organized, logical progression of ideas. Likewise, they are inappropriate in all varieties of written English except the most informal (as in letter-writing between close acquaintances): the pre-planning of formal speech is even more in evidence in the written medium, with the immediate availability of self-correction and re-writing.

Productive drills may be developed for some of the other grammatical features described above. A set of sentence connectives might be introduced into various sequences of sentences, e.g. *actually*, *in fact*, *unfortunately*, etc. within pairs such as *The train arrived on time. There weren't many people on it.* Conversely, one might be given an opening sentence followed by a connective, and the task is then to complete the second sentence, e.g. *Mary's older than my sister. Actually, . . .* In like manner, students might be asked to provide an appropriate response to a stimulus sentence, e.g. *A. Are you going to be at home tomorrow? B. Well actually, . . .* In all such exercises, it is important to ensure that the tenses of the two sentences are compatible. It is not possible to have, for example, *John came in at*

3 o'clock. Frankly, he's looking better, unless the second sentence is interpreted as parenthetic—that is, not intended to follow logically on from the first. The second sentence must be in the same tense-form as the first, or must use a tense-form implying an earlier time-reference, e.g. *Frankly I hadn't expected him/wasn't expecting him/ wouldn't have known him*. Lastly, one could introduce materials on the use of ellipsis—for example, by providing stimulus questions to which sentences in full and reduced form could be applicable, e.g. *John said he was going to the station in the morning. B. To where? A. To the station* (or *The station*, etc.).

4. There are many other interesting problems posed by a consideration of the material in the extracts; as indicated already, a number of questions remain unanswered. The student who is interested in doing some work of a descriptive linguistic or stylistic kind might therefore find some of the following questions worth investigating.

(i) What detailed restrictions upon the usage of connectives are there? For example, are there word-class restrictions following *sort of*? Are there preferences for certain types of phrase following *you know*? What are the exact tense-restrictions after *frankly*, etc.? How often does one have to make concomitant syntactic changes when a connective is omitted?

(ii) Compare and contrast the formality effects between two pieces of discourse, in which the only difference is in the use of connectives.

(iii) The tape illustrates a wide range of permissible intonation patterns, and in our analysis we have talked about 'normal' patterns with connectives. But what is the range of intonational variation permitted on these phrases? May one use *any* intonation? Or are there definite restrictions?

(iv) Set up a stimulus-response dialogue situation using a particular pair of sentences. Introduce various initial connectives, and examine the changes in the semantic relationship between the sentences. Can you develop a more sophisticated classification than our gross oppositions of reinforcing, diminishing, etc.? (Some suggestions about this may be found in Quirk *et al.*, Chapter 8.)

(v) Take one of the extracts and attempt to write it out in normal orthography. How easy is this? In particular, what punctuation problems arise? How acceptable, stylistically, is the resulting written English? What changes would be made in order to make it more acceptable in written form?

(vi) Can you find any regional differences in the use of connectives, softeners, etc.? If there are informants available, study the American softeners, such as *I guess*, using the same approach as in Chapter 3.

(vii) Contrast the informal language of these extracts with the language of any textbook on English you have used. How closely does the textbook correspond to colloquial English as represented here? Does it claim to? How consistent is it?

(viii) What cultural information may be obtained from the extracts? What is there in the language of the speakers to show that they are middle-class, educated, well-off, etc.?

(ix) Compare the dialogue of these extracts with the carefully constructed dialogues of such playwrights as Pinter, Wesker, and Osborne.

Bibliography

Abercrombie, D. 'Conversation and Spoken Prose'. *English Language Teaching*, **18**, 1963, 10–16.

Argyle, M. *Social Interaction*. London, Methuen, 1969.

Birdwhistel, R. L. *Kinesics and Context*. London, Allen Lane, 1971.

Crystal, D. *Prosodic Systems and Intonation in English*. London, C.U.P., 1969.

Crystal, D. and Davy, D. *Investigating English Style*. London, Longman, 1969.

Dickenson, L. and Mackin, R. *Varieties of Spoken English*, London, O.U.P., 1969.

Ervin-Tripp, S. M. 'An Analysis of The Interaction of Language, Topic and Listener'. In J. Gumperz and D. Hymes (eds.), *The Ethnography of Communication*, special number of *American Anthropologist*, **66**, 1964, 86–102.

Gimson, A. C. *An Introduction to the Pronunciation of English*, 2nd edn., London, Arnold, 1970.

Goldman-Eisler, F. 'Sequential Patterns and Cognitive Processes in Speech'. *Language and Speech*, **10**, 122–32.

Hendricks, W. O. 'Current Trends in Discourse Analysis'. In B. Kachru and H. Stahlke (eds.), *Current Trends in Stylistics*, Edmonton, Linguistic Research Inc., 1973.

Laver, J. and Hutcheson, S. (eds.), *Communication in Face-to-face Interaction*. Harmondsworth, Penguin, 1972.

Quirk, R., Greenbaum, S., Leech, G. and Svartvik, J. *A Grammar of Contemporary English*. London, Longman, 1972.

Robinson, W. P. *Language and Social Behaviour*. Harmondsworth, Penguin, 1972.

Sacks, H. *Social Aspects of Language: the Organization of Sequencing in Conversation*. Englewood Cliffs, Prentice-Hall, in press.

Schegloff, E. A. 'Sequencing in Conversational Openings'. In *American Anthropologist*, **70**, 1968, 1075–95.

Soskin, W. F. and John, V. 'The Study of Spontaneous Talk'. In R. G. Barket (ed.), *The Stream of Behavior*. New York, Appleton-Century-Crofts, 1963.

Index